holiday crafts
UNDER $10

Get in gear for a year of holiday fun! From Valentine's Day to Christmas, Holiday Crafts Under $10 *is your all-occasion guide to eye-catching decorations and accessories at unbelievably low prices. This volume in our Clever Crafter series is jam-packed with more than 90 extraordinary projects made with ordinary, inexpensive supplies. You'll find crafty ways to add pizzazz to your home, your table, and your wardrobe for rock-bottom prices (some for less than $2!). Combine the joy of celebrating with the excitement of creating extra-special centerpieces, wall hangings, embellished clothing, and other mementos. The key to organizing a nifty year of holiday happiness — with money to spare — is right at your fingertips!*

Anne Childs

LEISURE ARTS, INC.
Little Rock, Arkansas

holiday crafts UNDER $10

EDITORIAL STAFF

Vice President and Editor-in-Chief: Anne Van Wagner Childs
Executive Director: Sandra Graham Case
Editorial Director: Susan Frantz Wiles
Publications Director: Kristine Anderson Mertes
Creative Art Director: Gloria Bearden
Senior Graphics Art Director: Melinda Stout

DESIGN
Design Director: Patricia Wallenfang Sowers
Designers: Katherine Prince Horton, Sandra Spotts Ritchie, Anne Pulliam Stocks, Linda Diehl Tiano, and Rebecca Sunwall Werle
Executive Assistants: Debra Smith and Billie Steward

EDITORIAL
Managing Editor: Linda L. Trimble
Associate Editors: Karen A. Walker and Janice Teipen Wojcik
Assistant Editors: Tammi Williamson Bradley, Terri Leming Davidson, and Darla Burdette Kelsay
Copy Editor: Laura Lee Weland

TECHNICAL
Managing Editor: Sherry Solida Ford
Senior Technical Writer: Laura Lee Powell
Technical Writers: Carol V. Rye, Briget Julia Laskowski, and Leslie Schick Gorrell

ART
Book/Magazine Graphics Art Director: Diane M. Hugo
Senior Production Graphics Artist: Michael A. Spigner
Photography Stylists: Beth Carter, Pam Choate, Sondra Daniel, Laura Dell, Aurora Huston, and Courtney Frazier Jones

PROMOTIONS
Managing Editors: Alan Caudle, Tena Kelley Vaughn, and Marjorie Ann Lacy
Associate Editors: Steven M. Cooper, Dixie L. Morris, and Jennifer Leigh Ertl
Designer: Dale Rowett
Art Director: Linda Lovette Smart
Production Artist: Leslie Loring Krebs
Publishing Systems Administrator: Cindy Lumpkin
Publishing Systems Assistant: Susan Mary Gray

BUSINESS STAFF

Publisher: Bruce Akin
Vice President, Marketing: Guy A. Crossley
Vice President and General Manager: Thomas L. Carlisle
Retail Sales Director: Richard Tignor
Vice President, Retail Marketing: Pam Stebbins

Retail Marketing Director: Margaret Sweetin
Retail Customer Service Manager: Carolyn Pruss
General Merchandise Manager: Russ Barnett
Vice President, Finance: Tom Siebenmorgen
Distribution Director: Rob Thieme

CLEVER CRAFTER SERIES

Library of Congress Catalog Number 97-73653
International Standard Book Number 1-57486-118-2

Table of Contents

Table of Contents

ALL-AMERICAN DAYS 42

HALLOWEEN 54

Table of Contents

VALENTINE'S DAY

*L*ove is in the air on Valentine's Day! Those of us who are romantics at heart make the most of this special time to share thoughts of love and friendship; and it's only natural to dress our homes for the occasion, too. With our collection of charming home accents and tokens of affection, you can make the day especially memorable for those you hold dear. Whether you deliver flowers in a decorated vase or candy in a colorful wrap, the recipients will know your gifts came from the heart because you cared enough to craft them yourself. And since the pieces are so inexpensive to make, you'll have even more fun playing Cupid!

Let your love shine through the windows of your home with our sweet tree! An ideal Valentine's Day decoration at less than $10, this precious piece will tug at your heartstrings during the most romantic time of the year. Adorned with valentines and letters of love, the endearing project is also accented with conversation heart candies and wired-ribbon bows. (See instructions on pages 8 and 9.)

FIRST-CLASS CANDY

UNDER $5!

WHAT TO BUY

¹/₄ yd red fabric
³/₁₆"w picot-edged ribbon
(6-yd spool)
Three 1.55-oz. chocolate bars

THINGS YOU
HAVE AT HOME

White poster board, paper-backed fusible web, white paper, pinking shears, fabric scraps, black felt-tip pen, and glue

TECHNIQUES
YOU'LL NEED

Fusing Basics (pg. 104)

Deliver your valentines first-class! Snuggled in rich red fabric casings, our covered candy bars are lovingly stamped and addressed to your dearest ones. Deliciously inexpensive, three of these chocolate treasures can be given out for a dollar each!

COVERED CANDY BARS

1. Fuse web to wrong side of red fabric. For each candy bar, cut a 4³/₄" x 6" rectangle from fabric. Cut a 5¹/₄" x 6" rectangle from white paper. Center and fuse fabric piece to white paper piece. Use pinking shears to trim long edges of paper. Use pen to draw dots along cut edges of paper. Wrap cover around candy bar and glue in place.

2. For tag, cut 3" x 4" rectangles from fabric, web, and poster board. Fuse fabric to poster board. Use pinking shears to trim edges of tag.

3. Cut a 2" x 2³/₄" rectangle from poster board. Glue ends of a 7" ribbon length to back of poster board. Center and glue to tag.

4. Use "G" or "H" pattern (pg. 108) to make desired stamp or heart appliqué. Fuse appliqué to tag.

5. Center and glue tag to front of covered candy bar.

SWEETS FOR THE SWEET

WHAT TO BUY

1/4 yd red print fabric
5/8 yd each of two 3/4"w
    coordinating ribbons
3/16"w picot-edged ribbon
    (6-yd spool)
5/8 yd 3/8"w lace
Four 3" x 8" clear cellophane
    gift bags
16-oz. bag peppermint taffy

THINGS YOU
HAVE AT HOME

White poster board, paper-backed
fusible web, tracing paper,
pinking shears, 3/4"w web tape,
craft knife, cutting mat, glue,
buttons, and black felt-tip pen

TECHNIQUES
YOU'LL NEED

Making Patterns (pg. 104)
Fusing Basics (pg. 104)

Nothing beats sweets for the sweet! For a heartfelt touch, dress up our simple candy bags with fabric-covered poster board valentines trimmed with ribbons and lace.

CANDY GIFT BAGS

1. Fuse a 10" square of fabric to poster board. Cut four 5" squares each from fabric-fused poster board and remaining plain poster board.

2. Fuse web tape to 20" lengths of ribbon and lace. Cut ribbon and lace each into four 5" lengths. Fuse ribbons and lace to fabric-covered squares.

3. Use tracing paper to make "C" heart pattern (pg. 108). For each heart, use a pencil to lightly draw around pattern on fabric-covered square; cut out hearts along drawn lines. Glue each heart to a plain poster board square. Leaving a 1/4" border, use pinking shears to cut around hearts. Use pen to draw dots along cut edges of paper.

4. Use craft knife to cut two 1/4"l slits 1/2" apart at center of each heart.

5. Cut four 17" lengths of picot-edged ribbon. Thread ends of one ribbon length through slits to front of each heart. Glue a button to each heart.

6. Fill each bag with candy. Gather top of bag and insert through ribbon loop at back of each heart. Tighten ribbon and tie into a bow.

GIFT BOXES ABLOOM

WHAT TO BUY

Two 4" x 6" white gift boxes
1/8 yd red fabric
1/4"w green satin ribbon
(10-yd spool)

**THINGS YOU
HAVE AT HOME**

Tracing paper, buttons, and glue

**TECHNIQUES
YOU'LL NEED**

Making Patterns (pg. 104)

Help a young one craft a pretty gift box and watch the smiles blossom! A plain white package is transformed into a pleasant surprise by gluing fabric hearts and ribbon into the form of a cheery bloom.

GIFT BOXES

1. Use tracing paper to make "G" and "H" heart patterns (pg. 108).

2. For each box, use patterns to cut five "G" and four "H" hearts from fabric.

3. Cut one 12" and one 15½" ribbon length. Glue 2" of 12" ribbon length to center front of box lid and 3" of 15½" ribbon length to center of box bottom.

4. Arrange and glue large hearts in flower shape over ribbon end on top of box. Glue a button to center of flower.

5. Glue small hearts on box.

6. Tie ribbons into a bow.

PAINTSTITCHED PILLOW

Expect to Spend

fabric	1.69
interfacing	.27
paint	1.67
lace	1.15
fiberfill	1.72
Total	**$6.50**

*D*rift back to an age of childlike innocence, when romance was true and love was simple and pure, with our "redwork" pillow. Delicately painted with the look of embroidery stitches, a little girl with an apronful of valentines offers sweet sentiments to you from this eyelet-edged piece.

REDWORK PILLOW

1. Cut an 8" x 11 1/2" white fabric piece for pillow front and a 10 1/2" x 14 1/2" white fabric piece for pillow back. Center pillow front over pattern (pg. 107). Use a pencil to lightly trace design onto pillow front.

2. Cut an 8" x 11 1/2" piece of interfacing; fuse to wrong side of pillow front.

3. Follow manufacturer's instructions to paint over lines of design and to expand paint.

4. For borders, cut two 2" x 8" and two 2" x 14 1/2" strips from red fabric. Using 1/4" seam allowances, stitch short strips to top and bottom edges of pillow front. Stitch long strips to side edges of pillow front. Press seam allowances toward darker fabric.

5. Matching gathered edge of lace to raw edges of pillow front, pin lace to right side of pillow front; baste in place.

6. Pin pillow front and back right sides together. Using a 1/4" seam allowance and leaving an opening for turning, sew pillow front and back together. Clip corners; turn right side out and press, being careful not to touch iron to paint.

7. Stuff pillow with fiberfill; sew opening closed.

VALENTINE VASES

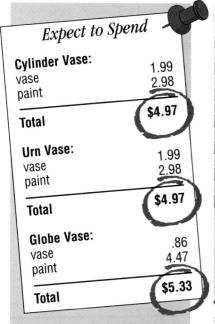

Expect to Spend

Cylinder Vase:	
vase	1.99
paint	2.98
Total	**$4.97**
Urn Vase:	
vase	1.99
paint	2.98
Total	**$4.97**
Globe Vase:	
vase	.86
paint	4.47
Total	**$5.33**

WHAT TO BUY

Tall cylindrical clear glass vase
Clear glass urn vase
Fluted-edge clear glass globe vase
Red, green, and black acrylic
   enamel paint

THINGS YOU HAVE AT HOME

Tracing paper, removable tape,
and paintbrushes

TECHNIQUES YOU'LL NEED

Making Patterns (pg. 104)
Painting Tips (pg. 105)

*B*ouquets of fragrant blossoms
will mean all the more when they're
delivered in one of our valentine
vases! By merely painting playful
hearts, charming buds, and scribbles
of sweetness, you can personalize
gifts for much less than a florist shop
would charge.

VALENTINE VASES

1. Use tracing paper to make desired patterns (pgs. 17 and 107).

2. Tape patterns inside vases.

3. Moving patterns for desired placement of designs, paint designs on outside of vases.

LOVE'S IN THE BAG

Expect to Spend

bags	.80
ribbon	3.10
felt	.20
pen	.97
Total for 4 bags	**$5.07**

WHAT TO BUY

Four white lunch-size gift bags
2 yds 1¹/₂"w black grosgrain
   ribbon
Red felt piece
Red felt-tip pen

THINGS YOU
HAVE AT HOME

Tracing paper, black felt-tip pen,
and glue

TECHNIQUES
YOU'LL NEED

Making Patterns (pg. 104)

*These versatile bags will "tie" up
special tokens for all your favorite
people! For a very reasonable cost,
you can fashion white paper bags
into a stylish shirt front for Dad,
handwrite sweet nothings on some,
or simply add hearts and ribbons.*

SWEET TALK BAGS

1. Use tracing paper to make "F" heart
pattern (pg. 108). Use pattern to cut two
hearts from felt.

2. To make two bags, use black pen to
write words on each bag. Use red pen to
draw hearts between words. Place gifts in
bags.

3. Fold top of each bag down ¹/₂"; repeat.
Staple bag at center of fold.

4. Cut two 23" lengths of ribbon. Tie each
length of ribbon into a bow; trim ends in
a "V" shape. Glue a bow to each bag.

5. Glue one heart to knot of each bow.

(Continued on page 17)

SWEETHEART VEST

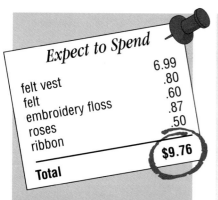

WHAT TO BUY

Adult-size ecru felt vest
Ecru, pink, red, and green felt
   pieces
One skein each of ecru, pink,
   and red embroidery floss
One package pink ribbon roses
1/8"w white satin ribbon
   (10-yd spool)

THINGS YOU HAVE AT HOME

Tracing paper, paper-backed
fusible web, embroidery needle,
and buttons

TECHNIQUES YOU'LL NEED

Fusing Basics (pg. 104)
Embroidery Stitches (pg. 106)
   Blanket Stitch

Charm your sweetheart (and friends, too) with our fun felt valentine vest! Appealing appliqués and a sprinkling of colorful buttons make the ready-made garment look especially nice.

VALENTINE VEST

1. Use patterns (pg. 108) to make desired heart appliqués.

2. Arrange appliqués on vest and fuse in place.

3. Use six strands of red floss to work Blanket Stitch along edges of vest and several hearts. Use floss or ribbon to work desired embroidery stitches along edges of remaining appliqués.

4. For each felt bow, cut a 1¼" square from ecru felt. Wrap a length of ecru floss tightly around middle of square. Sew a small button over center of bow and attach bow to vest.

5. Tie a 24" length of ribbon into a double-loop bow.

6. Use coordinating floss to sew bow, ribbon roses, and buttons to vest.

HEART-TO-HEART WREATH

WHAT TO BUY

¹/₈ yd each of white solid, white
   print, red print, and plaid
   fabric
¹/₂ yd pink print fabric
Polyester fiberfill (12-oz. bag)
10" dia. wooden embroidery hoop

THINGS YOU HAVE AT HOME

Paper-backed fusible web, white
paper, and white sewing thread

TECHNIQUES YOU'LL NEED

Making Patterns (pg. 104)
Fusing Basics (pg. 104)

Give someone a "hearty"
thank you *for her devotion with
our engaging valentine wreath! A
sentimental reminder of the strong
bond between friends, the piece is
fashioned by sewing six patchwork
pillows together — forming a ring of
love that's sure to be cherished.*

HEART-TO-HEART WREATH

1. Cut one 2¹/₂" x 18" white solid fabric
strip, two 1³/₄" x 18" plaid strips, twelve
1³/₄" x 5" white print strips, twelve
1³/₄" x 5" pink print strips, twelve
1¹/₂" x 7¹/₂" pink print strips, and six
7" x 7¹/₂" pink print rectangles.

2. (**Note:** For all sewing steps, match right
sides and raw edges, use a ¹/₄" seam
allowance, and press seam allowances to
one side.) Sew 18" white strip between 18"

(Continued on page 17)

HEARTFELT CARD HOLDER

Expect to Spend

felt	2.38
fabric	1.25
ribbon	1.11
paint	2.94
embroidery floss	.20
dowel	.29
Total	**$8.17**

WHAT TO BUY

¹/₄ yd each of ecru and pink felt
3 green felt pieces
¹/₄ yd large floral print fabric
1 yd ¹/₄"w pink ribbon
³/₁₆"w ecru picot-edged ribbon
    (6-yd spool)
Iridescent pink and green
    dimensional paint
Green embroidery floss
¹/₄" dia. dowel rod

THINGS YOU HAVE AT HOME

Tracing paper, paper-backed
fusible web, pinking shears, glue,
embroidery needle, and handsaw

TECHNIQUES YOU'LL NEED

Fusing Basics (pg. 104)
Painting Tips (pg. 105)
Embroidery Stitches (pg. 106)
    Blanket Stitch
    Running Stitch

Now you can keep those special valentines close to your heart with our charming felt card holder. Pastel hearts accented with floral fabric appliqués create beautiful pockets for you to display your mementos.

FROM THE HEART CARD HOLDER

1. Cut an 8¹/₂" x 29" rectangle of pink felt for backing. Cut 7¹/₂" x 28¹/₂" rectangles of ecru felt and web for pocket background; cut three 7¹/₂" ecru felt squares for pocket fronts.

2. Using pinking shears to cut out appliqués, use "A" pattern (pg. 108) to make three heart appliqués from pink felt. Fuse one pink heart to each green felt

(Continued on page 17)

16

LOVE'S IN THE BAG
(Continued from page 13)

HEARTS BAG

1. Use tracing paper to make "E" and "F" heart patterns (pg. 108). Use patterns to cut two small hearts and one large heart from felt.

2. Place gift in bag. Fold top of bag down 1"; repeat. Staple bag at center of fold.

3. Cut a 9" length of ribbon. Trim ends in a "V" shape. Glue ribbon diagonally to bag over fold. Cut a 13" length of ribbon; overlap ends 1/2" to form a loop; glue in place. Center and glue loop over diagonal ribbon. Glue large heart to center of loop. Glue small hearts to bag.

NECKTIE BAG

1. Use tracing paper to make "F" heart pattern (pg. 108). Use pattern to cut one heart from felt.

2. Cut top 3 1/2" from the front and sides of bag. Cut back of bag into two points to make collar.

3. Tie one end of a 12" ribbon length into a necktie knot; trim opposite end to a point. Glue to top front of bag.

4. Glue heart to bag.

5. Place gift in bag; fold points over front of bag to look like a shirt collar.

HEART-TO-HEART WREATH
(Continued from page 15)

plaid strips to make strip set. Cut across strip set at 2 1/2" intervals to cut six pieced units.

3. For each block, sew one white print strip to each long edge of pieced unit, then sew one 1 3/4" x 5" pink print strip to each end of pieced unit. Sew one 1 1/2" x 7 1/2" strip to each long edge of pieced unit to complete block. Make six blocks.

4. Use "F" pattern (pg. 108) to make six heart appliqués from red print fabric. Center and fuse one appliqué to white square in center of each block.

5. Use tracing paper to make "A" heart pattern (pg. 108).

6. For each stuffed heart, place one block and one pink print rectangle right sides together. Center heart pattern on wrong side of rectangle and draw around pattern. Leaving an opening for turning, sew pieces together directly on drawn line. Cut out, leaving a 1/4" seam allowance. Clip seam allowance at curves and at cleft of heart; turn right side out and press. Stuff heart with fiberfill; sew opening closed by hand.

7. Arrange stuffed hearts in a circle and sew edges together to form a wreath; place wreath wrong side up on flat surface. Center inner solid hoop of embroidery hoop on back of wreath; whip stitch in place.

HEARTFELT CARD HOLDER
(Continued from page 16)

piece. Use pinking shears to cut each green heart 1/4" larger than pink heart. Make three appliqués from floral fabric.

3. Center and fuse appliqués on pocket fronts. Using pinking shears and leaving a 1/4" ecru border, cut top edge of each pocket into a heart shape. Use dimensional paint to paint edges and add detail lines to floral appliqués.

4. Center and fuse pocket background to backing. Spacing pockets evenly on pocket background, use six strands of floss to work Blanket Stitch along side and bottom edges of each pocket.

5. For rod pocket, fold top edge over 1 1/2" and use six strands of floss to work Running Stitch through all layers 1 1/4" from top of card holder.

6. For hanger, use handsaw to cut a 9 1/2" length of dowel. Insert dowel through rod pocket. For each bow, cut two 15" lengths of pink and ecru ribbon; tie together into a bow. Cut an 18" length of ecru ribbon. Tie ends around ends of dowel; glue in place. Glue one bow to each end of dowel over ribbon.

ST. PATRICK'S DAY

There's a magical spirit surrounding St. Patrick's Day — one that conjures up images of sprightly leprechauns who lead us over rainbows in search of sparkling pots o' gold! Bring a touch of Irish wonder to your home with our delightful collection of projects. From clovers to charms, our decorative pieces will enchant your holiday guests, while our fun favors give St. Paddy's Day partygoers a twinkling of luck. Our creations are so inexpensive, you can spend your day playfully pinching those who forget their green — instead of pinching pennies!

You'll have the luck of the Irish on your side with our whimsical St. Patrick's Day centerpiece — a piece of good fortune for less than $10! Cheery little leprechauns and pots of gold hang from the tiny tree, next to bags of Irish luck full of glimmering foil-wrapped "coins." Paper shamrock cutouts and penny decorations make nifty accents. (See instructions on pages 23, 24, and 25.)

IRISH COFFEE MUGS

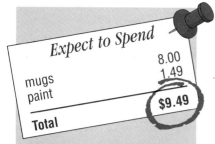

WHAT TO BUY

Two white Irish coffee mugs
Green DecoArt™ Ultra Gloss
acrylic enamel paint

THINGS YOU HAVE AT HOME

Tracing paper, transfer paper,
stylus, tape, and a small
paintbrush

TECHNIQUES YOU'LL NEED

Making Patterns (pg. 104)
Painting Tips (pg. 105)

Hail three hearty cheers for Lady Luck with our set of Irish coffee mugs! A cinch to decorate, plain white cups are painted with a trail of hearts and clovers. These cute mugs are worth their weight in gold!

IRISH COFFEE MUGS

1. (**Note:** We recommend hand washing painted mugs after use.) Transfer entire pattern (this page) to side of one mug; reverse pattern and transfer to opposite side of other mug. Transfer four hearts to handle and one heart to pedestal of each mug.

2. Paint transferred designs green and paint green stripes on pedestals.

SHAMROCK AND HEARTS

GENTLE BLESSING TABLE TOPPER

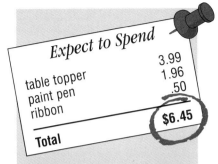
WHAT TO BUY

30" dia. white lace-edged table
  topper
Green paint pen
1/4"w green picot-edged ribbon
  (6-yd spool)

THINGS YOU
HAVE AT HOME

Drawing compass, tracing paper,
transfer paper, stylus, and pencil

TECHNIQUES
YOU'LL NEED

Making Patterns (pg. 104)
Painting Tips (pg. 105)

*B*ring the gentle blessings of
Ireland into your home with our
embellished table topper. To make
this pretty piece, simply use a paint
pen to write in the center and along
the edges of a purchased cloth.
Painted shamrocks and green ribbon
finish off this economical accent.

IRISH TABLE TOPPER

1. Use compass to lightly draw a 5" dia.
circle at center of table topper. Transfer
grouped shamrocks pattern (pg. 27) to
center of circle.

2. Referring to "An Irish Blessing" verse
(this page), use a pencil to lightly write

words along edge of topper; transfer small
shamrock pattern (pg. 27) between
phrases.

3. Use paint pen to paint words and
shamrocks green.

4. Weave a length of ribbon through holes
in lace and tie ends into a bow.

An Irish Blessing

May the road rise up to meet you,
May the wind be always at your back,
May the sun shine warm upon your face,
And the rain fall soft upon your fields,
And until we meet again,
May God hold you in the palm of His
  hand.

21

SHAMROCK BANNER

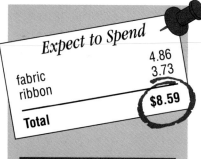

WHAT TO BUY

Fabric:
- ³/₄ yd muslin for background
- ¹/₃ yd shamrock floral for borders
- ¹/₈ yd each of three green prints
- ¹/₈ yd brown print
- 4¹/₃ yds ⁷/₈"w green grosgrain ribbon

THINGS YOU HAVE AT HOME

³/₄"w fusible web tape, paper-backed fusible web, tracing paper, buttons, black sewing thread, and an approx. 1¹/₄" dia. x 30"l stick

TECHNIQUES YOU'LL NEED

Fusing Basics (pg. 104)

*Y*our friends will be green with envy when they see this beautiful banner in your home! Fashioned from festive prints, the fused project is amazingly inexpensive. What a fun and easy way to celebrate your happy fortune!

ST. PATRICK'S DAY WALL HANGING

1. Wash, dry, and press fabrics and ribbon without using fabric softener.

2. Fuse web to wrong side of each fabric except muslin. Fuse web tape to ribbon.

3. For wall hanging front, cut a 26" square from muslin. Cut four 3" x 26" strips and five 3" x 7¹/₂" rectangles for tabs from fabric for borders, and two ¹/₂" x 6" strips

from each fabric for shamrock stems. Do not remove paper backing from border strips.

4. Press long edges of border strips 1" to wrong side. Remove paper backing. Insert one side edge of wall hanging front into one fold of border strip with wide edge to front; fuse in place. Repeat for remaining side edge, then for top and bottom edges.

5. For ribbon borders, cut ribbon into six 24" lengths. Arrange and fuse two ribbon lengths, one vertically and one horizontally, across center of wall hanging front; fuse remaining ribbons 1⁷/₈" from each side edge, then top and bottom edges of wall hanging front.

(Continued on page 27)

LUCKY CHARMS

Expect to Spend

fabric	1.95
photocopies	1.00
chocolate coins	3.00
ribbon	.50
paper	.10
tissue paper	.20
Total	**$6.75**

WHAT TO BUY

1/4 yd of muslin
1/4 yd green print fabric
Six photocopies of label (pg. 27)
Six 5/8-oz. bags of chocolate coins
1/8"w green satin ribbon
    (10-yd spool)
One sheet green construction
    paper
Green tissue paper

THINGS YOU HAVE AT HOME

Ecru sewing thread, colored
pencils, tapestry needle, empty
can (we used a 6" dia. x 4 1/2"h
mixed nuts can), white poster
board, tracing paper, paper-
backed fusible web, and glue

TECHNIQUES YOU'LL NEED

Making Patterns (pg. 104)
Fusing Basics (pg. 104)

Dazzle guests with these lucky charms to make your St. Patrick's Day bash rich in fun! Muslin sacks are filled with candy coins and adorned with photocopied labels that you color with pencils. Our shamrock tin makes a clever holder for the favors, as well as a creative centerpiece.

PARTY FAVOR CENTERPIECE

1. For each bag, cut a 7" square of muslin.

2. Fold muslin square in half. Leaving one end (top of bag) unstitched, use a 1/4" seam allowance to sew remaining edges together. Clip corners and turn bag right side out.

3. Fold top of bag 1 1/2" to inside; press.

4. Use colored pencils to color photocopy of label (pg. 27). Cut out and glue label to front of bag.

5. Fill bag with candy coins, reserving one coin for Step 7.

(Continued on page 27)

LEPRECHAUN MAGNETS

WHAT TO BUY

Plaid™ 8-color acrylic paint set
Gold metallic paint
1/2"w self-adhesive magnetic strip
(30" roll)

THINGS YOU HAVE AT HOME

Tracing paper, white poster board, transfer paper, stylus, paintbrushes, white and black acrylic paint, black permanent felt-tip pen, and glue

TECHNIQUES YOU'LL NEED

Making Patterns (pg. 104)
Painting Tips (pg. 105)

UNDER $5!

The holiday wouldn't be the same without rosy-cheeked leprechauns popping up in unexpected places. This fun figure is merely cut from poster board and painted. The cost of making a half-dozen magnets is so low, you won't believe your luck!

LEPRECHAUN MAGNETS

1. Use tracing paper to make leprechaun patterns (pg. 108). Draw around patterns on poster board. Cut up to six shapes from each pattern.

2. Basecoat hat green, face peach, and beard red.

3. Transfer hat, face, and beard details to shapes.

4. Paint over details on shapes. Use pen to outline painted areas and draw facial features. Use white paint to add highlights to hat, eyes, and cheeks.

5. Glue face to beard and hat to face.

6. Cut a 1 1/2" length of magnetic strip and attach to back of each leprechaun.

POT OF GOLD MAGNETS

WHAT TO BUY

Gold metallic paint
1/8"w green satin ribbon
  (10-yd spool)
1/2"w self-adhesive magnetic strip
  (30" roll)

THINGS YOU HAVE AT HOME

Tracing paper, white poster board, transfer paper, stylus, paintbrushes, white and black acrylic paint, black permanent felt-tip pen, and glue

TECHNIQUES YOU'LL NEED

Making Patterns (pg. 104)
Painting Tips (pg. 105)

Finding that elusive pot of gold will be a cinch at your house! Glittering with metallic paint, our fanciful magnet is perfect for posting reminders of special activities. Since six magnets cost less than $3, you'll want to share the wealth with a buddy or two!

POT OF GOLD MAGNETS

1. Use tracing paper to make pot of gold patterns (pg. 109). Draw around patterns on poster board. Cut up to six shapes from each pattern.

2. Basecoat front piece and back piece of pot black; basecoat coin piece metallic gold.

3. Transfer detail lines of coin pattern to coin piece.

4. Paint gold and white highlights on front of pot. Use pen to draw over detail lines and white paint for highlights on coin piece.

5. Glue coin piece to top of back piece; glue front piece of pot to back piece.

6. Tie a 9" length of ribbon into a bow; glue bow to front of pot and glue ends of bow to back.

7. Cut a 1 1/2" length of magnetic strip and attach to back of pot.

BLARNEY STONE

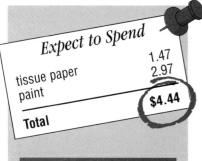
WHAT TO BUY

One package green tissue paper (our package included five different shades of green)
White, red, and green acrylic paint

THINGS YOU HAVE AT HOME

A clean smooth rock, acrylic spray sealer, paintbrushes, tracing paper, glue, foam brush, transfer paper, stylus, and black permanent felt-tip pen

TECHNIQUES YOU'LL NEED

Making Patterns (pg. 104)
Painting Tips (pg. 105)

*G*et ready for a "rocking" St. Patrick's Day with our nifty, thrifty Blarney stone! This collage of clover is cleverly crafted by gluing green tissue paper cutouts to a painted rock. With its playful pucker and endearing request for kisses, this shamrock-covered stone makes a great paperweight or a novel good-luck charm!

BLARNEY STONE

1. Spray rock with sealer; allow to dry.

2. Paint rock green.

3. Use tracing paper to make shamrock pattern (this page). Use pattern to cut several shamrocks from each shade of tissue paper.

4. Thin glue with water to consistency of ink. Using foam brush to apply glue, attach shamrocks to rock.

5. Transfer lips pattern (this page) to rock. Basecoat lips red. Mix a small amount of white paint with red paint and paint highlights on lips.

6. Shade lips by drawing a line with pen and quickly smudging with finger. Use pen to outline lips and shamrocks and to add details.

7. Use white paint to write "Kiss Me" on rock.

8. Spray rock with sealer.

LIPS

SHAMROCK

26

SHAMROCK BANNER
(Continued from page 22)

6. In each square on wall hanging front, arrange and fuse two matching 1/2" x 6" fabric strips in an "X."

7. Use patterns (this page and pg. 108) to make twelve "F" heart appliqués from each green fabric and sixteen leaf appliqués from brown fabric. Matching fabrics, arrange and fuse three heart appliqués over each end of shamrock stems; fuse leaf appliqués between shamrocks.

8. For tabs, press each long edge of each tab rectangle to center; remove paper backing and fuse in place. Use buttons to sew ends of tabs over top of wall hanging. Sew remaining buttons to center of each appliqué.

9. Insert stick through tabs.

LEAF

IRISH LUCK LABEL

LUCKY CHARMS
(Continued from page 23)

6. Thread needle with a 12" length of ribbon. Take a stitch through center of bag 1" from top. Tie ends of ribbon into a bow at front of bag.

7. Glue remaining coin just inside top of bag.

8. Measure around can and add 1"; measure height of can. For can cover, cut a piece of poster board the determined size.

9. Fuse web to wrong side of fabric piece. Adding 1" to height, cut fabric piece the size of can cover. Fold long edges of fabric 1/2" over can cover; fuse in place.

10. Use tracing paper to make pattern (this page) for each section of three shamrocks. Fold green paper along lines accordion-style (**Fig. 1**), then cut out shamrock shape. Glue sections to can cover 1/2" from top, trimming as needed.

Fig. 1

SHAMROCK GROUP

11. Cut a 7" length of ribbon for each shamrock on can; tie each length into a bow. Glue a bow below each shamrock stem.

12. Wrap cover around can and glue overlapping ends together.

13. Place tissue paper and "Irish Luck" bags in can.

SHAMROCK

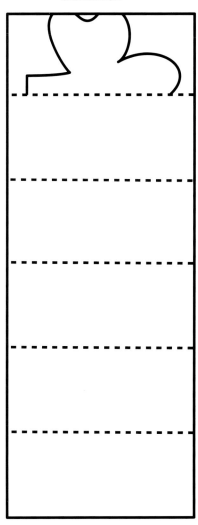

Leisure Arts, Inc., grants permission to the owner of this book to photocopy the label design on this page for personal use only.

EASTER

The spring sunshine warms our souls, stirring us into thoughtful reflection of the true meaning of Easter. We venture outdoors to behold nature's renewal, breathing in the freshness of it all. Traditions such as bunnies and baskets of candy are cheerful celebrations of the day, and our playful projects are a fun way to bring them to life! Using simple materials to fashion a variety of adorable accents, you can decorate your entire home — from tabletops to doors to windows — for practically pennies! Or spread cheer to "somebunny" special with a charming gift bag full of tasty treats. Our pretty pieces are so amazingly inexpensive that you'll have a spring in your step and a smile on your face as you craft your way through the Easter holiday!

Brighten your favorite nook with the sunny colors of spring! For less than $10, you can create a cute country table tree using several darling designs from our Easter collection. Vivid paper carrots and playful jelly bean daisies (they're used to decorate a flowerpot and gift bags later) adorn this seasonal centerpiece — tempting the taste buds of our funny egghead bunnies. These whimsical projects will fill your home with Easter excitement! (See pages 32, 33, and 39 for instructions.)

FENCEROW RABBITS

WHAT TO BUY

White, yellow, and pink acrylic paint
4"w green and light purple paper twist (6-yd packages)
One 28¹/₂" long white wooden fencing piece
One stem artificial flowers

THINGS YOU HAVE AT HOME

Tracing paper, white poster board, transfer paper, stylus, paintbrushes, black permanent felt-tip pen, and glue

TECHNIQUES YOU'LL NEED

Making Patterns (pg. 104)
Painting Tips (pg. 105)

*C*elebrate the traditional *Easter egg hunt with our darling door hanging! Simply cut and paint bunny and egg shapes from poster board, and then glue each one to a length of white wooden fencing. Artificial flowers and paper-twist bows add springtime spirit!*

BUNNIES IN THE TRELLIS

1. Use tracing paper to make bunny head and egg patterns (pgs. 109 and 110).

2. Use patterns to cut three bunnies and seven eggs from poster board.

3. Basecoat bunnies white and eggs white, yellow, and pink. Paint desired designs on eggs.

4. Transfer detail lines to bunnies. Paint mouth, inner ears, and nose pink. Use pen to color eyes and to draw over transferred lines.

5. For bows, cut three 20" lengths of light purple paper twist and untwist. Tie each length into a bow; set aside.

6. Remove six flowers from stem. For each leaf, cut a 3" length of green paper twist. Holding one end for stem of leaf, untwist opposite end; trim into a leaf shape.

7. Arrange bunnies, eggs, bows, leaves, flowers, and a length of green paper twist for vine on fence; glue in place.

TABLETOP EASTER BASKET

WHAT TO BUY

¹/₃ yd fabric
Jumbo craft sticks (75 pack)
8"w paper twist (6-yd pack) to
   coordinate with fabric
One stem artificial flowers
Easter grass

THINGS YOU HAVE AT HOME

Shoe box or similar box, utility
scissors, white acrylic paint,
paintbrush, thread, and glue

TECHNIQUES YOU'LL NEED

Painting Tips (pg. 105)

Transform an ordinary shoe box into a delightful centerpiece using our easy-to-follow steps. Paper twist forms the handle and bows, and jumbo craft sticks create the look of a picket fence. Fill the box with Easter grass, nestle in a few colored eggs, and you have a splendidly affordable accent for a beautiful holiday brunch!

EASTER BASKET CENTERPIECE
(**Note:** The Easter basket is for decorative purposes only.)
1. Measure around box; add ¹/₂". Measure height of box; add 3". Cut a piece of fabric the determined measurements.

2. Matching one long edge of fabric with bottom edge of box, glue fabric piece around box; turn down excess fabric and glue to inside of box.

3. For each picket, use utility scissors to cut one end of craft stick straight and the other end into a point. Paint pickets white. Spacing evenly, glue pickets to outside of box.

4. For handle length, measure from bottom edge of one end of box to bottom edge of opposite end of box, allowing for arch of handle (**Fig. 1**); multiply by three. Cut three lengths of paper twist the determined measurement.

Fig. 1

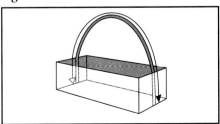

(Continued on page 41)

CUTE CARROT FLOWERPOT

Expect to Spend

clay pot	.68
paint	.99
fabric	1.50
paper twist	1.38
floss	.20
ribbon	.50
bunny	3.99
Total	**$9.24**

WHAT TO BUY

6"h clay pot
White acrylic paint
¼ yd fabric
6"w orange and green paper twist
Brown embroidery floss
¼"w satin ribbon (10-yd spool)
10½"h stuffed bunny

THINGS YOU
HAVE AT HOME

Matte acrylic spray sealer,
paintbrush, glue, foam brush,
and aluminum foil

TECHNIQUES
YOU'LL NEED

Painting Tips (pg. 105)

*You'll have a hippity-hoppity
good time this Easter making
our cute carrot flowerpot tended
by a precious plush rabbit. The
painted, fabric-covered clay pot is
highlighted with a row of irresistible
carrots easily made from foil and
paper twist.*

CARROT FLOWERPOT

1. Spray pot with sealer. Paint inside of pot
and outside of rim white.

2. To cover pot, cut four 4½" x 5½"
pieces of fabric. Mix one part glue with one
part water. Use foam brush to apply glue
mixture to pot evenly below rim. Place
fabric pieces on flowerpot wrong side
down, overlapping to cover pot below rim;
smooth in place. Working from center
outward, gently smooth any wrinkles or
bubbles in fabric with brush. Fold and glue
extra fabric to bottom of pot. Brush glue
mixture over fabric; allow to dry.

3. For each carrot, cut a 3" x 6" piece of
foil. Form foil into carrot shape.

4. For roots on each carrot, cut three 3"
lengths of floss; place lengths together and
fold in half. Glue fold of roots to bottom tip
of foil carrot.

(Continued on page 41)

JELLY BEAN DAISY BAGS

WHAT TO BUY

12-oz. bag large jelly beans
Seven white 6" x 11" gift bags
Yellow, green, and purple curling
 ribbon (66-ft spools)
Seven sheets pink or purple tissue
 paper

THINGS YOU HAVE AT HOME

Tracing paper, poster board,
paper-backed fusible web,
drawing compass, fabric scraps
for leaves, hole punch, and glue

TECHNIQUES YOU'LL NEED

Fusing Basics (pg. 104)

For less than $1, you can transform a paper bag into a "delectable" delight using a handful of jelly beans and some curling ribbon. Just glue the candies into a flower shape, and then add a few leaves made from fabric-covered poster board.

JELLY BEAN DAISY BAGS

1. For cuff on bag, fold top of bag down 3/4"; fold down again 1 1/4". Punch an even number of holes around cuff of bag.

2. Use leaf pattern (pg. 110) to make fabric appliqués.

3. Fuse appliqués to poster board; cut out.

4. Use compass to draw a 1 1/2" dia. circle on poster board; cut out. Glue jelly beans to circle in a flower shape. Glue leaves and flower to bag.

5. Thread three 48" lengths of ribbon through holes in cuff and tie into a bow at front of bag; curl ends. Line bag with tissue paper.

DARLING DRESS

WHAT TO BUY

Child-size T-shirt
5/8 yd fabric for skirt
White medium rickrack
White, yellow, light purple, and
   green acrylic paint
3/8"w satin ribbon (6-yd spool)

THINGS YOU HAVE AT HOME

Fabric marking pen, ruler, sewing
thread, tracing paper, transfer
paper, stylus, T-shirt form or
cardboard covered with waxed
paper, straight pins, paintbrushes,
black permanent felt-tip pen, and
a felt scrap for chick's beak

TECHNIQUES YOU'LL NEED

Making Patterns (pg. 104)
Painting Tips (pg. 105)

Wearing a new outfit is as much a part of Easter tradition as chocolate bunnies and jelly beans! For a mere $10, you can make your favorite little girl feel extra special by sewing up our quick-and-simple dress for her. Fashioned by adding a skirt to a purchased tee, this rickrack-accented piece is festively adorned with colorful eggs and a baby chick — all easily painted using transferred patterns!

EASTER DRESS

1. Wash and dry shirt, fabric, and rickrack without using fabric softener; press.

2. For bodice, use fabric marking pen and ruler to draw a line across shirt 7 3/4" from shoulder seams. Lay shirt flat; cut off bottom of shirt along drawn line. Baste around bottom of shirt.

3. (**Note:** Use a 3/8" seam allowance unless otherwise indicated.) For skirt, cut a 20" x 44" piece of fabric. Matching right sides and short edges, sew short edges together; press seam allowance open. Baste 1/4" from one long raw edge of skirt. Pull basting threads to gather skirt to fit bottom of bodice. Knot threads.

4. Matching right sides and raw edges, and placing skirt seam at center back of bodice, pin skirt to bodice, adjusting gathers evenly. Stitch in place. Press seam allowance toward bodice.

5. For hem, press bottom edge of skirt 1/2" to wrong side; press 1" to wrong side again. Stitch in place.

6. For cuffs, turn each sleeve up 1/2"; repeat and press. Cut a length of rickrack to fit around cuff. Center rickrack over cuff edge and stitch in place. Cut a length of rickrack to fit along front neck ribbing from shoulder seam to shoulder seam plus 1/2". Turning under 1/4" at each end, center

rickrack over edge of ribbing and stitch in place. Cut a length of rickrack to fit around bodice seam; stitch in place over seam.

7. Transfer pattern (pg. 41) to bodice front. Reverse unbroken eggs pattern and transfer to bottom of dress.

8. Place dress on T-shirt form. Paint designs on dress. Use pen to outline eggs, chick, and eyes. Draw eyebrows and color irises in chick's eyes. Paint white highlights in chick's eyes.

9. For beak, cut a 1/4" square of felt. Finger press felt square in half diagonally. Hand stitch along fold to attach beak to chick.

10. Cut two 24" lengths of ribbon and tie each into a bow. Sew bows to dress.

SOFT-TOUCH SWITCH PLATES

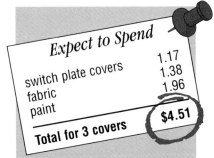

Expect to Spend

switch plate covers	1.17
fabric	1.38
paint	1.96
Total for 3 covers	**$4.51**

WHAT TO BUY

Three switch plate covers with smooth surfaces
Three 1/8-yd fabric pieces
Pastel acrylic paint set with eight colors

THINGS YOU HAVE AT HOME

Fabric marking pen, craft knife, cutting mat, glue, foam brush, tracing paper, transfer paper, stylus, fabric scrap for daisy appliqués, buttons, white poster board, and paintbrushes

TECHNIQUES YOU'LL NEED

Making Patterns (pg. 104)
Painting Tips (pg. 105)

Light up your Easter with our soft pastel switch plates! You can make three covers for less than $5 — a brilliant bargain. Each features a darling design that's easy to create from our patterns. They're so pretty and practical, you'll want to use them year round!

FABRIC-COVERED SWITCH PLATE

1. Measure switch plate height and width. Add 1" to both measurements. Cut a piece of fabric the determined measurements.

2. Place fabric wrong side up; center switch plate on fabric. Use fabric marking pen to draw around switch plate and opening at center of switch plate. Draw lines connecting opposite corners of switch opening.

3. Cut outside corners at an angle. Use craft knife to cut along diagonal lines just to outline for switch opening (**Fig. 1**).

Fig. 1

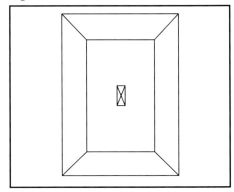

(Continued on page 41)

PERKY TABLE RUNNER

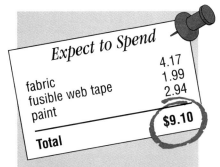
WHAT TO BUY

44"/45"w fabric:
- ⁵⁄₈ yd large pink check for center of runner
- ¹⁄₄ yd small pink check for wide borders
- ¹⁄₃ yd white for bunnies
- ¹⁄₈ yd small green check for narrow borders and bow ties
- ¹⁄₈ yd pink for inner ears and noses
- ¹⁄₈ yd black for eyes and mouths

³⁄₄"w fusible web tape

White and black dimensional paint

THINGS YOU HAVE AT HOME

Paper-backed fusible web

TECHNIQUES YOU'LL NEED

Fusing Basics (pg. 104)
Painting Tips (pg. 105)

*O*ur adorable runner will perk up your table! Three little bunnies all in a row wish you a "hoppy" Easter on this no-sew project, which is charming for any springtime celebration.

BUNNY RUNNER
Finished Size: 16¹⁄₂" x 52¹⁄₂"

1. Cut an 18" x 44¹⁄₂" piece from fabric for center of runner. Cut two 3¹⁄₈" x 18" strips of fabric for narrow borders. Cut two 10¹⁄₂" x 18" pieces of fabric for wide borders.

2. Fuse web tape along short ends on wrong side of center fabric piece. Overlap one end of center fabric piece ³⁄₄" over one long edge of one wide border fabric piece and fuse in place. Repeat for remaining end of center fabric piece.

3. For each narrow border, fuse a length of web tape along each long edge on right side of one fabric strip. Do not remove paper backing. Press edges to wrong side along inner edge of tape. Remove paper backing. Center narrow border strip over seam between center and wide border fabric pieces and fuse in place.

4. For hem, fuse web tape along long edges on wrong sides of table runner. Do not remove paper backing. Press edges to wrong side along inner edge of tape. Unfold and remove paper backing; refold and fuse in place. Repeat to hem ends of runner, pressing ends 5³⁄₄" to wrong side of runner.

5. Use bunny head, inner ears, eyes, nose, mouth, and bow tie patterns (pg. 110) to make six appliqués each. Arrange three sets of appliqués at each end of runner and fuse in place.

6. Use black paint to outline bow ties, ears, eyes, nose, and mouth and to paint whiskers and remainder of mouth. Use white paint to outline bunnies.

EASTER SUN CATCHERS

WHAT TO BUY

One package of six 8" x 10" clear
shrink art plastic sheets (we
used Aleene's Clear
Shrink-It™ Plastic)
Black dimensional paint
White tissue paper (10 pack)
Assorted watercolor markers
One package Mill Hill small bugle
beads (#72051 - Royal
Mauve)

THINGS YOU HAVE AT HOME

Removable tape, glue, foam
brush, hole punch, and clear
nylon thread

TECHNIQUES YOU'LL NEED

Making Patterns (pg. 104)

*Invite the springtime sun to
dance through your windows! By
decoupaging tissue paper onto
shrinkable plastic, you can make
eight spectacular sun catchers for
just under $10.*

EASTER SUN CATCHERS

1. Place plastic over patterns (pgs. 109 and
110); tape in place. Use dimensional paint
to draw outlines of designs; allow to dry.

2. Mix one part glue to one part water. Use
foam brush to apply glue mixture to back
of plastic.

3. Place tissue paper over glue and smooth
in place. Use markers to color designs as
desired; allow to dry. Apply a second coat
of glue mixture over colored designs.

4. Punch a hole in the top of each
ornament. For each hanger, cut an 8"
length of clear thread. Fold in half and
thread looped end through hole in
ornament. Bring both ends of thread
through the loop and pull ends tightly
against sun catcher. String eight beads onto
each end of thread. Tie into a knot close to
beads; trim thread ends.

FUNNY BUNNIES

WHAT TO BUY

4"w white and pink paper twist
(6-yd packages)
Five white foam eggs
Ten 10mm oval wiggle eyes
White and brown embroidery floss
7/8 yd 2"w white flat lace trim
1/2 yd 5/8"w grosgrain ribbon
Yellow, green, and purple curling
ribbon (66-ft spools)
Five 2" x 8 1/2" clear pleated
cellophane gift bags
Two 12-oz. bags jelly beans

THINGS YOU HAVE AT HOME

Floral wire, wire cutters, and glue

O ur funny bunnies offer a sweet "Happy Easter" to all! Simply silly, these sacks of colorful jelly beans are topped with adorable foam egg bunny heads. Craft a whole family with toothy grins, lace collars, and embroidery floss hair!

EGGHEAD BUNNY BAGS

1. (**Note:** Follow Steps 1 - 6 for each bunny.) For ears, cut a 7 1/2" length of white paper twist and a 7" length of pink paper twist. Untwist paper twist lengths; line white paper with pink paper. Slightly roll edges of white paper over pink paper. Fold ends together to resemble tips of rabbit ears and glue to secure. Fold ears into a "V" shape. Glue ears to small end of egg.

2. Glue two wiggle eyes to egg. For nose, glue a small piece of crumpled pink paper twist below eyes. For whiskers, cut four 3" lengths of white floss; glue below nose. For teeth, cut two 1/4" lengths of white paper twist; glue below whiskers.

3. For hair, cut three 2" lengths of brown floss, fold in half and glue to top of head; separate strands.

4. For collar, cut a 5 1/2" length of lace. Weave floral wire through top of lace. Gather lace tightly on wire and twist to secure; trim wire ends close to lace. Glue to bottom of head.

5. For tie, cut a 3" length of grosgrain ribbon. Pinch at center and glue to head above collar.

6. Fill gift bags with jelly beans; tie with curling ribbon and curl ends. Glue bunnies to tops of bags.

EGGSHELL MOSAIC FRAMES

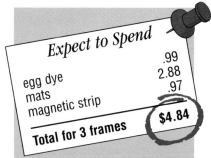

Expect to Spend

egg dye .99
mats 2.88
magnetic strip .97

Total for 3 frames **$4.84**

WHAT TO BUY

Easter egg dye kit
Three 5" x 7" precut mats
¹/₂"w self-adhesive magnetic strip
(30" roll)

THINGS YOU HAVE AT HOME

Eggshells, chlorine bleach, glue,
matte acrylic spray sealer, photos
to fit in mats, lightweight
cardboard, and tape

UNDER $5!

*Show off unforgettable moments
in our one-of-a-kind picture frames!
Glue dyed eggshell pieces onto a
precut mat to create a marvelous
mosaic of your own design. And
since they're so affordable, you can
easily whip up a whole dozen!*

MOSAIC FRAMES

1. (**Caution:** Wear rubber gloves and work
in a well-ventilated area when working with
bleach.) Thoroughly rinse eggshells in
water. Place shells in jar and cover with a
solution of one part bleach and one part
water. Place lid on jar and allow shells to
soak at least 24 hours. Remove shells from
jar and place on paper towel to dry.

2. Follow manufacturer's instructions to
dye eggshells desired colors. Break shells
into small pieces.

3. Cover a small area of mat with a layer
of glue. Carefully press shells into glue,
arranging in desired pattern. Continue
until mat is covered.

4. Spray dried mat with 2 to 3 coats of
sealer.

5. For backing, cut a 5" x 7" piece of
cardboard. Center photo in frame opening
and tape in place. Glue backing to frame.
Attach lengths of magnetic strip to back of
frame.

TABLETOP EASTER BASKET
(Continued from page 31)

5. Beginning and ending 3" from ends of paper twist, braid handle. Knot a length of thread around each end of braid to secure.

6. Cut two 18" lengths of paper twist; untwist. Tie each length into a bow.

7. Glue handle, bows, and flowers to ends of box.

8. Line box with Easter grass.

CUTE CARROT FLOWERPOT
(Continued from page 32)

5. For carrot top, cut a 4" length of green paper twist; untwist. Make 1/4"w cuts along one long edge of paper to within 1" of opposite edge. Cut a 4" length of orange paper twist; untwist. Glue uncut edge of carrot top to short edge of orange paper twist. Roll around foil carrot; glue in place.

6. For bow, cut a 12" length of ribbon and tie around base of carrot top.

7. Repeat steps 3 - 6 to make nine carrots. Glue eight carrots around covered flowerpot. Place bunny and one carrot in flowerpot.

SOFT-TOUCH SWITCH PLATES
(Continued from page 36)

4. Use foam brush to coat front of switch plate with glue. Center switch plate on wrong side of fabric and smooth fabric in place. Fold edges of fabric over edges of switch plate and glue in place.

5. Use a craft knife to make small cuts in fabric at openings for screws.

TULIP SWITCH PLATE

1. Transfer tulip pattern (this page) to covered switch plate.

2. Paint tulips. Paint screwheads to coordinate with tulips and fabric.

DAISY SWITCH PLATE

1. Use tracing paper to make daisy pattern (this page). Use pattern to cut two daisies from fabric. Glue daisies to covered switch plate.

2. Paint screwheads to coordinate with fabrics.

3. Glue buttons to covered switch plate.

EASTER EGG SWITCH PLATE

1. Use tracing paper to make egg pattern (this page). Use pattern to cut three eggs from poster board.

2. Paint eggs. Paint screwheads to coordinate with fabric.

3. Glue eggs to covered switch plate.

ALL-AMERICAN DAYS

Show your red-white-and-blue spirit this summer with our star-spangled All-American Days collection! Whether you're marveling at a sparkling fireworks display on Independence Day, cheering at a Memorial Day Parade, or waving our nation's colors on Flag Day, this spectacular montage of inexpensive projects is sure to fire up your patriotic pride! Spice up a backyard barbecue with red-hot picnic accessories, or hail a colorful salute to our servicemen and women by donning festive duds. You could even honor your grass roots heritage by filling your home with a wealth of star-studded decorations. But what makes our collection particularly patriotic is the care that goes into crafting each project. Pride in workmanship is an all-American quality that you will feel when making these eye-catching creations!

Our patriotic pieces make a colorful collage — perfect for an all-American tree! The branches of this amazingly affordable adornment are brightened by firecracker favors, while patchwork blocks and button-trimmed stars make charming country complements. Add a few inexpensive items of your own, such as a string of popcorn, and you have a sizzling centerpiece for less than $10! (See pages 45, 48, and 49 for instructions.)

CONSTITUTIONAL COZY

Expect to Spend

drink cozy	2.59
transfer pen	3.49
buttons	1.70
Total	**$7.78**

WHAT TO BUY

Natural canvas drink cozy (we used a Bagworks™ cozy with blue binding)
Iron-on transfer pen
Two 3/4" dia. red buttons

THINGS YOU HAVE AT HOME

Tracing paper or white paper, black permanent felt-tip pen, red acrylic paint, paintbrush, and red sewing thread

TECHNIQUES YOU'LL NEED

Making Patterns (pg. 104)
Painting Tips (pg. 105)

*Y*ou'll be all wrapped up in fireworks and fun with our cool constitutional cozy! While the padded canvas cover keeps your drink frosty, it also boasts of our true-blue American freedom. Easy and inexpensive, the wrap is a patriotic way to sit and sip away the summer!

CONSTITUTIONAL DRINK COZY

1. Follow pen manufacturer's instructions to transfer pattern (pg. 111) to drink cozy.

2. Use permanent pen to draw over lowercase letters in design.

3. Paint star and uppercase letters in design red.

4. Use red thread to sew buttons 1/2" inside edge of cozy on side opposite loop fastener.

FIRECRACKER FAVORS

WHAT TO BUY

Fabric:
   ¹/₄ yd red and white stripe
   ¹/₈ yd blue and white print
White chenille stems (25 pack)
Wrapped candies
Red wired star garland (25 ft)

THINGS YOU HAVE AT HOME

Foam paintbrush, empty toilet tissue rolls, and glue

*H*ost a bang-up celebration with these red-hot firecracker favors! You'll marvel at the spectacularly low cost of making a set of eight for less than $5 — and impress party guests with your creativity! Simply glue striped and print fabrics to "recycled" toilet tissue rolls to fashion the firecrackers, then fill them with wrapped candies.

FIRECRACKER FAVORS

1. For each favor, cut a 5¹/₂" x 9" piece of striped fabric and a 2" x 5¹/₂" piece of blue print fabric.

2. Use foam brush to apply glue to empty toilet tissue roll. Center roll along one long edge of striped fabric piece. Smooth fabric around roll; glue fabric at overlap.

3. Press long edges of blue fabric piece ¹/₄" to wrong side. Matching one pressed edge with one end (top) of roll and overlapping ends, glue blue fabric piece around fabric-covered roll.

4. Cut two 4" lengths of chenille stem. Twist one 4" length around fabric at bottom of roll and push end of fabric into tube.

5. Fill firecracker with candy.

6. For fuse, cut two 6" lengths of star garland and fold in half. Twist one end of remaining 4" chenille stem length around fabric to close top of firecracker; twist other end around center of star garland pieces.

45

SPECTACULAR TEE

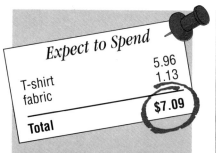
WHAT TO BUY

Child-sized T-shirt (ours was purchased with patriotic print sleeves)
¹/₈ yd each of blue solid and print fabrics for star appliqués
¹/₈ yd red solid fabric for banner appliqué

THINGS YOU HAVE AT HOME

Paper-backed fusible web, tear-away stabilizer, tracing paper, transfer paper, stylus, white acrylic paint, paintbrush, clear nylon thread, white thread, and buttons

TECHNIQUES YOU'LL NEED

Fusing Basics (pg. 104)
Painting Tips (pg. 105)
Stitched Appliqués (pg. 105)

F rom feasting on red, ripe watermelon to romping in the July sun, your child will have more fun playing her holiday away wearing our stars and stripes T-shirt. Appliqués and buttons dress up a white tee, making it festive garb for your little firecracker. And at a cost of around $7, you'll have change left for a few extra surprises!

"GOD BLESS AMERICA" T-SHIRT

1. Use patterns (pg. 113) to make one banner and four star appliqués.

2. Arrange appliqués on shirt and fuse in place.

3. Use clear thread to zigzag stitch appliqués in place.

4. Transfer pattern for words (pg. 113) to banner. Use white paint to paint over transferred lines.

5. Sew buttons to shirt.

STARS & STRIPES PILLOW

Expect to Spend

bandannas	1.98
fabric	3.49
fiberfill	3.44
Total	**$8.91**

WHAT TO BUY

Two flag-print bandannas
1/2 yd 60"w denim fabric
Two 12-oz. bags polyester fiberfill

THINGS YOU HAVE AT HOME

Sewing thread

Sink into the lazy days of summer with this plump patriotic pillow. Fashioned from flag-print bandannas and fringed with denim, this eye-catching cushion makes a dynamic accent.

PATRIOTIC BANDANNA PILLOW

1. For fringe, cut two 9" x 60" strips from denim fabric.

2. Matching wrong sides, press each strip in half lengthwise.

3. Matching pressed edges of denim strips with edges of one bandanna and butting ends of strips (do not overlap), pin denim strips to one bandanna, trimming to fit. Baste in place.

4. Matching right sides and edges and leaving an opening for turning, use a 1/2" seam allowance to stitch bandannas together. Turn right side out and press.

5. To fringe denim, make clips in denim 3/4" to 1" apart, clipping to edges of bandannas. To make denim fringe twist and ravel, wash and dry pillow cover. Trim threads.

6. Stuff pillow cover with fiberfill. Hand stitch opening closed.

FESTIVE FOURTH SWAG

WHAT TO BUY

Fabric:
- 1/4 yd muslin for quilt squares and stars
- 1/8 yd red check for quilt squares
- 1/8 yd blue print for quilt squares
- 1/4 yd blue star print for stars and bows

Ecru felt piece
Natural jute twine (3-ply)
Two 4 1/2" x 6 1/2" American flags
3 1/2-ft-long grapevine swag

THINGS YOU HAVE AT HOME

Tracing paper, paper-backed fusible web, poster board, black permanent felt-tip pen, buttons, and glue

TECHNIQUES YOU'LL NEED

Fusing Basics (pg. 104)

*T*his festive swag will make your mantel sizzle and pop! With its unfurled flags, rustic stars, and quilt blocks, the thrifty project is a salute to our nation's pioneer heritage.

FESTIVE 4TH SWAG

1. Follow Steps 3 - 8 of **Quilt-Block Snack Savers** instructions (pgs. 49 and 53) to make two Ohio Star and three Pinwheel ornaments.

2. For each ornament hanger, cut two 6" lengths of jute. Knot one end of each length. Knot the two lengths together at opposite ends. Glue small knots to top corners of ornament.

3. For stars, fuse muslin to poster board. Use pattern (pg. 113) to make three star appliqués. Fuse appliqués to muslin-covered poster board; cut out stars 1/4" outside appliqués. Use pen to draw stitches along edges of stars.

4. Cut three 12" lengths of jute; tie each into a bow. Glue bow to center of each star; glue a button to each bow knot.

5. For fabric bows, tear three 1 1/2" x 12" strips of fabric and tie into bows.

6. Hang ornaments on swag. Glue flags, stars, and bows to swag.

STAR-SPANGLED SNACK SAVERS

Expect to Spend

containers	10.76
snack mix	11.96
fabric	2.11
felt	.20
jute twine	.99
Total for 4 containers	**$26.02**
Each container	**6.50**

WHAT TO BUY

Four 2-quart square plastic
    containers
Four 14-oz. bags snack mix
Fabric:
    1/8 yd each:
        muslin
        red check
        dark blue print
    1/4 yd blue print for lid covers
Ecru felt piece
Natural jute twine (3-ply)

THINGS YOU
HAVE AT HOME

Pinking shears, rubber bands,
buttons, paper-backed fusible
web, and glue

TECHNIQUES
YOU'LL NEED

Fusing Basics (pg. 104)

*N*o gathering is complete
without a ready supply of tempting
treats, and these spirited snack
savers are an ideal place to
store holiday eats! Accented
with quilt blocks, quaint buttons,
and simple bows, the canisters
display lots of country charm.
At less than $7 each, they're worth
an all-American salute!

QUILT-BLOCK SNACK SAVERS

1. Fill each container with snack mix and
replace lid.

2. For each lid, use pinking shears to cut
an 8 1/2" square of light blue fabric. Place
fabric square over lid and secure with a
rubber band. Tear a 1" x 20" strip from red
fabric. Fold in half lengthwise and wrap
around lid, covering rubber band; knot at
front. Glue button over knot.

3. For ornaments, fuse web to wrong side
of red fabric. Fuse muslin to felt piece.

4. For each ornament, cut a 4" square from
red fabric. Cut a 3 1/2" square from felt-
fused muslin.

5. For each Ohio Star quilt block, use
patterns (pg. 111) to make Ohio Star and
small square appliqués. Arrange appliqués
at center of one muslin square and fuse in
place.

6. For each Pinwheel quilt block, use
pattern (pg. 111) to make four Pinwheel
appliqués. Arrange appliqués on one
muslin square and fuse in place.

(Continued on page 53)

SPIRITED UNCLE SAM

WHAT TO BUY

Fabric:
  1/2 yd for background
  3/8 yd for border and shirt
  1/8 yd each for stars appliqués,
    pants appliqué, hat
    appliqué, and hanger tabs
Buttons:
  Three 7/16" dia. for jacket
  Two 5/8" dia. gold for epaulets
  Three 7/8" dia. for tabs
7/16" dia. dowel rod
Red dimensional paint

THINGS YOU
HAVE AT HOME

Lightweight fusible interfacing,
paper-backed fusible web, fabric
scraps for remaining appliqués,
black permanent felt-tip pen, red
pencil, buttons, glue, handsaw,
white acrylic paint, and a
paintbrush

TECHNIQUES
YOU'LL NEED

Making Patterns (pg. 104)
Fusing Basics (pg. 104)
Painting Tips (pg. 105)

Celebrate Independence Day with grand old Uncle Sam! From his striped top hat to his star-spangled trousers, he brings a folksy cheeriness to this banner. Quite a bargain at less than $10, this star-studded wall hanging is guaranteed to make your summer sensational!

UNCLE SAM BANNER

1. For background, cut 17" x 23" rectangles of background fabric and interfacing. Fuse interfacing to wrong side of fabric.

2. For borders, fuse web to a 13" x 35" piece of fabric. Cut two 4" x 17" strips and two 4" x 23" strips from fused fabric. Do not remove paper backing.

3. Press border strips in half lengthwise. Remove paper backing. Insert one long edge of background fabric into one long border strip; fuse in place. Repeat for remaining long edge, then short edges of banner.

4. Use patterns (pgs. 112 and 113) to make Uncle Sam and star appliqués. Arrange and fuse appliqués to background fabric.

(Continued on page 53)

QUILTER'S FLAG T-SHIRT

WHAT TO BUY

Adult-sized red T-shirt
Fabric:
   ¹/₈ yd each of solid red,
      blue print, red check,
      and muslin
   ¹/₄ yd star print
   ³/₈ yd ticking

THINGS YOU HAVE AT HOME

Paper-backed fusible web, tear-away stabilizer, clear nylon thread, sewing thread, and buttons

TECHNIQUES YOU'LL NEED

Fusing Basics (pg. 104)
Stitched Appliqués (pg. 105)

Your heart will swell with pride when you show your spirit in this brightly colored tee! Adorned with a beautiful pieced Ohio Star in one corner, the appliquéd flag is a fitting tribute to the birth of our nation.

OHIO STAR FLAG T-SHIRT

1. Use patterns (pg. 111) to make Ohio Star appliqué. Fuse web to wrong sides of remaining fabrics. Do not remove paper backing.

2. For flag appliqué, cut a 9" x 13" piece of ticking. Cut the following appliqués from remaining fabrics: one 5¹/₂" square from star print fabric, one 4¹/₄" square from solid red fabric, one 3" square from muslin, and one 1¹/₂" square from red checked fabric.

3. Arrange and fuse square and star appliqués to one corner of flag appliqué. Remove paper backing from flag appliqué and fuse to shirt.

4. Stitch appliqués in place.

5. For cuffs, turn sleeves up 1"; repeat and press. Sew buttons along cuffs and front neck ribbing.

PATRIOTIC PICNIC BASKET

Expect to Spend

basket	3.96
fabric	2.67
batting	.40
ribbon	2.61
Total	**$9.64**

WHAT TO BUY

Basket (ours measures 10" x 18")
  with handle
1 yd red check fabric
1/4 yd low-loft batting
1 3/4 yds 1"w blue ribbon
1 1/2 yds 1"w red ribbon (or
  enough to fit around basket
  rim)

THINGS YOU
HAVE AT HOME

Corrugated cardboard, paper-
backed fusible web, fabric scraps
for star appliqués, poster board,
buttons, and glue

TECHNIQUES
YOU'LL NEED

Making Patterns (pg. 104)
Fusing Basics (pg. 104)

*As all-American as Mom,
baseball, and apple pie, this patriotic
picnic basket is sure to put the Yankee-
Doodle dazzle into your Fourth of July
festivities! Our red, white, and blue
ruffle and tie-on lid add sparkle to an
inexpensive basket — creating a picnic
pack that's perfect for carrying all your
holiday favorites.*

COVERED PICNIC BASKET
1. For basket lid, draw around each end of
basket on corrugated cardboard (**Fig. 1**).
Cut pieces from cardboard.

Fig. 1

2. For lid, cut two pieces from fabric 1 1/2"
larger on all sides than one cardboard
piece. Cut two pieces of batting same size
as one cardboard piece.

3. Use patterns (pg. 53) to make desired
number of star appliqués. Arrange on right
side of lid fabric pieces and fuse in place.

4. For lid lining, cut two pieces of poster
board same size as one cardboard piece.
Cut two fabric pieces 1" larger on all sides
than one poster board piece. Set lid lining
pieces aside.

5. To cover one side of lid, center one
batting piece, then one cardboard piece on
wrong side of one lid fabric piece.
Alternating sides and pulling fabric taut,
glue edges of fabric to cardboard. Repeat
for remaining side of lid.

6. For fabric hinge, measure width of
basket between ends of handle; add 1".
Measure width of handle; add 2 1/2". Cut two

(Continued on page 53)

STAR-SPANGLED SNACK SAVERS
(Continued from page 49)

7. To assemble each ornament, center one quilt block, right side up, on wrong side of one 4" red square. Fold edges of red square over edges of quilt block square and fuse in place.

8. Glue a button to center of each ornament.

9. For each hanger, cut two 12" lengths of jute. Knot one end of each length. Glue knots to top back corners of ornament. Tie ornament around container lid.

SPIRITED UNCLE SAM
(Continued from page 50)

5. Use pen to draw stitches along edges of stars and background fabric; draw a line down center of pants and dots for eyes. Use red pencil to color cheeks. Use dimensional paint to draw arm lines.

6. For hanger tabs, cut two fabric pieces and one web piece 4½" x 7"; fuse web between fabric pieces. Cut three 1¼" x 6" strips from fused fabric. Fold each strip in half to form a loop. Glue ends of loops to back of banner.

7. Glue buttons to jacket, epaulets, stars, and top border just below tabs.

8. Use handsaw to cut dowel rod 19½" long. Paint dowel white. Insert dowel through hanger tabs.

PATRIOTIC PICNIC BASKET
(Continued from page 52)

strips of fabric the determined size. Press short edges of each hinge strip ½" to wrong side. Cut blue ribbon in half. Fold each length in half and glue point to wrong side of hinge strip (**Fig. 2**).

Fig. 2

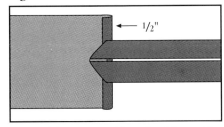

7. Matching wrong sides, glue hinge strips together along the edges.

8. Measure width of handle; add 1". Place padded lid pieces, wrong side up, with straight edges the determined distance apart. Center hinge over space between lid pieces and glue long edges of hinge to lid pieces (**Fig. 3**).

Fig. 3

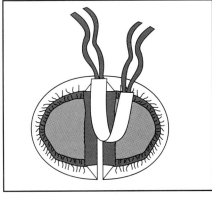

9. To cover each lid lining piece, center one poster board piece on wrong side of one fabric piece. Alternating sides and pulling fabric taut, glue edges of fabric to poster board. Glue one lining piece to wrong side of each lid piece.

10. For ruffle, measure around basket rim; multiply by two. Cut a 7"w strip of fabric the determined length, piecing if necessary. Press each short end of strip ½" to wrong side. Matching wrong sides, press strip in half lengthwise. Baste 1", then 2", from raw edges. Pull basting threads to gather ruffle to fit around the basket rim.

11. With basting line even with top of basket, glue ruffle in place. Glue top fabric edges to inside of basket. Glue red ribbon over fabric edges.

12. Place lid on basket (lid may have to be folded to fit through handle). Tie ribbons into bows around handle; trim ribbon ends. Glue buttons on streamer ends and on basket top.

HALLOWEEN

Witches and goblins and ghosts — oh my! What fun it is to fill your home with the delightful frightfulness of this bewitching time, when monsters of all ages don scary garb and gobble up terrific treats. Homemade decorations, gifts, and clothing add to the excitement of this harvesttime holiday — and save you dollars and cents to boot! A parade of spooky spirits dances through our Halloween section, promising to make merry mischief during this spine-tingling season. Projects range from "boo-tiful" to practical to practically petrifying. So turn the pages to learn how to scare up a batch of crafty goody bags and bony skeletons, but remember — no tricks allowed!

Create a new tradition for less than $10 — a Halloween tree to help your jack-o'-lantern guard the front door! Displayed in a painted coffee can, our twig tree is haunted by easygoing ghosts. Magnetic pumpkins and creative Halloween cans filled with colorful corn add to the fun. (See pages 56, 59, and 60 for instructions.)

CREATIVE HALLOWEEN CANS

What a smart idea! You can transform ordinary food cans into charming holders for Halloween goodies. Ours use simple supplies such as spray paint, craft foam, tissue paper, fabric, curling ribbon, and chenille stems. These environmentally friendly projects are extremely economical, too. Make up to five cans for less than $7.50 — and that includes treats to fill the smallest tins!

WHAT TO BUY

Green and black spray paint
One sheet each of white and
     orange craft foam
1/8 yd fabric
12 1/2-oz. package of candy corn
One spool each of yellow and
     black curling ribbon
     (66-ft spools)
One sheet each of orange, purple,
     and green tissue paper
Assorted chenille stems (25 pack)

THINGS YOU HAVE AT HOME

Small and medium cans (we used food cans and 3-oz. cat food cans); nail and hammer; tracing paper; transfer paper; stylus; craft knife; cutting mat; orange, green, and black felt-tip pens; yellow, dark green, and black acrylic paint; paintbrushes; coated floral wire; wire cutters; natural raffia; glue; plastic bags or plastic wrap; and buttons

TECHNIQUES YOU'LL NEED

Making Patterns (pg. 104)
Painting Tips (pg. 105)

BASIC CAN

1. Working from inside of can, use nail and hammer to punch holes in sides of can for handles.

2. Spray paint can green or black.

3. For handle, cut a 12" length of chenille stem. Twist center of chenille stem around a pencil to curl if desired. Thread ends of chenille stem through holes in can; twist to secure.

SKULL TREAT CAN

1. Use tracing paper to make skull pattern (pg. 70). Cut one skull from white foam.

2. Use black pen to draw mouth and cracks on skull. Glue skull to can.

3. Tear a 3/4" x 40" strip from fabric and tie into a bow around bottom of can.

4. Glue buttons to can. Line can with tissue paper.

PUMPKIN TREAT CAN

1. Follow Steps 1, 2, and 4 of **Jack-O'-Lantern Magnets** (pg. 60) to make foam pumpkin without a magnet.

2. Glue foam pumpkin to can. Glue buttons to can. Line can with tissue paper.

"TRICK OR TREAT" CAN

1. Cut a piece of orange foam to fit around can.

2. Use black pen to write "TRICK OR TREAT" at center of foam piece. Glue foam piece to can.

3. Tie a length of raffia into a bow; glue to top of foam piece.

4. Glue buttons to can. Line can with tissue paper.

GREEN CAN

1. Use tracing paper to make small pumpkin and ghost patterns (pg. 117). Cut two ghosts from white foam and two small pumpkins from orange foam.

2. Use colored pens to add details to pumpkins and black pen to draw faces on pumpkins and eyes on ghosts.

3. Fill plastic bag or plastic wrap with candy corn; tie with lengths of curling ribbon and curl ends.

4. Glue buttons to can.

SCARY PHOTO ALBUM

WHAT TO BUY

One 10" x 11½" photo album
⅓ yd low-loft batting
⅔ yd fabric to cover album
¼ yd orange fabric for
     background
1 yd ⅝"w purple grosgrain
     ribbon.
Four ¾" dia. yellow buttons
Black jumbo rickrack
     (2½-yd package)

THINGS YOU
HAVE AT HOME

Lightweight cardboard, tracing
paper, transfer paper, stylus,
4½" x 6" white and black fabric
pieces, paper-backed fusible web,
black permanent felt-tip pen,
white and black acrylic paint,
paintbrushes, ⅝"w fusible web
tape, glue, pressing cloth, and
raffia

TECHNIQUES
YOU'LL NEED

Making Patterns (pg. 104)
Fusing Basics (pg. 104)
Painting Tips (pg. 105)

*T is the season to be frightened!
Our suitably scary photo-keeper has
a warning label for those who dare to
look inside. Converting an ordinary
album into a monstrous memory-keeper
is a cinch! Just layer batting, fabric, and
trimmings and anchor them with glue
and fusible web.*

SCARY PHOTO ALBUM

1. Measure width and height of open
album. Cut a piece of batting the
determined size. Cut fabric piece 2" larger
on all sides than batting.

2. Glue batting to outside of closed album.
Center open album on wrong side of fabric
piece. Glue corners of fabric over corners
of album. Glue edges of fabric over edges
of album, trimming to fit around hardware.

3. Cut two cardboard pieces ½" smaller on
all sides than album front. Cut two fabric
pieces 1" larger on all sides than cardboard
pieces. Center one cardboard piece on
wrong side of one fabric piece. Glue
corners of fabric over corners of
cardboard. Glue edges of fabric over edges
of cardboard. Repeat to cover remaining
cardboard piece. Glue covered cardboard
pieces to inside front and back of album.

(Continued on page 70)

EASYGOING GHOSTS

UNDER $5!

WHAT TO BUY

¹/₂ yd white cotton fabric
Elmer's school glue (4 oz.)
6"h plastic foam cone (2 pack)

THINGS YOU HAVE AT HOME

Drawing compass, white paper, plastic wrap, aluminum foil, string, black felt-tip pen, needle, and clear nylon thread

Hide them in lunch boxes, hang them from trees or doorways, or perch them on desktops — you'll find lots of hot spots for these spooky spirits, which can be made for less than 50 cents! Simply stiffen a circle of fabric with glue and shape into a chilling design using a foil ball and string. Both children and adults will love creating these goblins.

GHOSTS

1. For pattern, use compass to draw an 8" dia. circle on paper; cut out.

2. For each ghost, use pattern to cut circle from fabric.

3. Wrap foam cone with plastic wrap.

4. For head, crumple a piece of foil into a 1" dia. ball.

5. Mix one part glue with two parts water. Dip fabric circle in glue mixture. Remove excess glue mixture.

6. Place foil ball at center of fabric circle. Tie an 8" length of string around fabric below foil ball at "neck." Place ghost on cone and arrange gathers in fabric; allow to dry. Remove ghost from cone.

7. Remove string from neck. Use pen to draw eyes on ghost.

8. For hanger, thread needle with a 6" length of clear thread. Take a stitch at top of head. Knot thread ends together.

MAGNETIC JACK-O'-LANTERNS

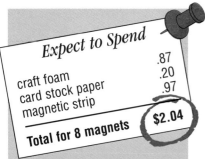
WHAT TO BUY

One sheet orange craft foam
8¹/₂" x 11" sheet of yellow card
   stock paper
¹/₂"w self-adhesive magnetic strip
   (30" roll)

THINGS YOU HAVE AT HOME

Tracing paper; yellow, dark green,
and black acrylic paint;
paintbrush; coated floral wire;
wire cutters; craft knife or
scissors; cutting mat; and glue

TECHNIQUES YOU'LL NEED

Making Patterns (pg. 104)
Painting Tips (pg. 105)

Wow! You can whip up eight crafty jack-o'-lantern magnets for only $2! Charming on your refrigerator or as colorful accents in ghoulish gift baskets, these toothsome designs are fashioned from craft foam. Friends and family will be really "attracted" to these nifty magnets.

JACK-O'-LANTERN MAGNETS

1. Use tracing paper to make pumpkin pattern (pg. 117). Cut shape from craft foam; cut eyes, nose, and mouth.

2. Paint pumpkin sections, stem, and leaves on foam shape.

3. Draw around pumpkin on yellow paper; cut out just inside drawn line. Glue paper piece to back of pumpkin.

4. Attach a 1" length of magnetic strip to back of pumpkin. For tendril, curl one end of a 5" length of floral wire around a pencil. Glue end of wire to back of pumpkin.

PUMPKIN-PATCH PULLOVER

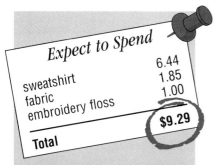
WHAT TO BUY

Adult-sized black sweatshirt
1/8 yd each of three orange fabrics
  and two green fabrics for
  appliqués
Three orange and two green
  skeins of embroidery floss

THINGS YOU HAVE AT HOME

Paper-backed fusible web,
embroidery needle, buttons, and
black sewing thread

TECHNIQUES YOU'LL NEED

Fusing Basics (pg. 104)
Embroidery Stitches (pg. 106)
  Blanket Stitch
  Running Stitch
  French Knots

*S*imple embroidered vines wind
down the sleeve of our loose-fitting
pumpkin appliqué sweatshirt. You can
make a seasonal fashion statement
(and chase away autumn chills) for
just over $9! The ribbing is removed
from the sweatshirt's neck, sleeves, and
waist to produce the fuller effect.

PUMPKIN-PATCH PULLOVER

1. Wash, dry, and press sweatshirt and
fabrics.

2. Cut ribbings from neck, bottom, and
sleeves of sweatshirt; cut sleeves 1/2" longer
than desired length.

3. Turn neck, bottom, and sleeve edges 1/2"
to wrong side and baste in place.

(Continued on page 70)

BONY SKELETON

Expect to Spend

dog bone treats	4.46
paint	1.49
chenille stems	.50
ribbon	.97
Total	**$7.42**

WHAT TO BUY

Box of small dog bone treats
Box of large dog bone treats
White spray paint
Large gauge white chenille stems
(25 pack)
1/3 yd 7/8"w ribbon

THINGS YOU HAVE AT HOME

Cardboard, paintbrushes, black acrylic paint, tracing paper, transfer paper, stylus, black felt-tip pen, heavy-gauge floral wire, wire cutters, and glue

TECHNIQUES YOU'LL NEED

Making Patterns (pg. 104)
Painting Tips (pg. 105)

This friendly fellow is hanging around hoping to frighten the socks off anyone brave enough to cross his path. Adding our skeleton to your Halloween decor costs less than $8! Merely paint an assortment of dog treats white, glue them to a chenille stem frame, and top them with a grinning cardboard skull.

BONY SKELETON

1. Paint fifteen small bones and four large bones white.

2. Use tracing paper to make skull pattern (pg. 70). Draw around pattern on cardboard; cut out. Paint skull white. Transfer eyes and nose to skull. Paint eyes and nose black. Paint white highlights in eyes. Use pen to draw mouth and cracks in skull.

(Continued on page 71)

GOBLIN DOOR HANGER

WHAT TO BUY

³/₈" dia. dowel
6"w orange paper twist
    (6-yd pack)
²/₃ yd white fabric
¹/₈ yd fabric for bow tie
One sheet each of yellow, green,
    and black craft foam
Red felt piece
1¹/₄ yds ¹/₈"w black satin ribbon
Two ³/₄" dia. white buttons
Photocopy of "Tricks" pattern
    (pg. 115) for sign

THINGS YOU HAVE AT HOME

Handsaw, newspaper, floral wire,
wire cutters, glue, pinking shears,
tracing paper, craft knife, cutting
mat, hole punch, and poster
board

TECHNIQUES YOU'LL NEED

Making Patterns (pg. 104)

*O*ur grinning ghost carries a
clear warning — "no tricks allowed!"
This $7 door decoration is quickly
assembled using wooden dowels for
support and newspaper-stuffed paper
twist for the jack-o'-lantern head.

HALLOWEEN DOOR DECORATION

1. Use handsaw to cut dowel rod into two
18" lengths.

2. For head, cut four 14" lengths of paper
twist; untwist paper lengths. Glue long
edges of lengths together, forming a tube.
For stem, use a 6" length of wire to close
tube 2" from one end. Stuff head with
newspaper. Insert dowel into center of
stuffed head. Secure head to dowel with a

wire length, leaving enough wire to form a
loop for hanger.

3. Use tracing paper to make mouth, nose,
and eye patterns (pg. 115). Cut shapes
from black foam. Glue to head.

4. For arms, place remaining dowel at base
of head; secure with a length of wire
wrapped in a crisscross manner around
dowels.

5. Use pinking shears to cut along one long
edge of white fabric. Gather fabric
2¹/₂" from pinked edge around neck of
pumpkin above arms. Secure gathers with a
length of wire. Drape fabric over arms and
glue in place.

(Continued on page 71)

ENCHANTING WITCH

Celebrate Halloween by making an enchanting centerpiece! Our raffia-haired witch, complete with broomstick and treat bag, is as appealing as she is economical. Her ghoulish green face is a carved foam egg covered with a sock, and a sand-filled soda bottle forms her body.

WHAT TO BUY

2³/₄" x 3⁷/₈" plastic foam egg
   (2 pack)
One pair of bright green socks
³/₈ yd fabric for dress and sleeves
¹/₃ yd black felt for cape
5" dia. felt witch's hat
Two 20mm oval wiggle eyes

THINGS YOU HAVE AT HOME

2-liter plastic beverage bottle with lid, sand or gravel to weight bottle, tracing paper, serrated knife, thin corrugated cardboard, aluminum foil, straight pin, ¹/₂"w fusible web tape, thread to match dress fabric, heavy-gauge floral wire, wire cutters, yarn scrap for cape tie, natural raffia, fabric scrap for hatband, poster board, yellow acrylic paint, paintbrush, black felt-tip pen, jute twine or string for bag handle, 8" long twig for broom, white paper for tooth, and glue

TECHNIQUES YOU'LL NEED

Making Patterns (pg. 104)
Fusing Basics (pg. 104)

TABLETOP WITCH

1. Fill bottle with sand or gravel to desired weight and replace lid.

2. Use tracing paper to make hand, nose, and star patterns (pg. 114).

3. For head, refer to **Fig. 1** and use serrated knife to remove section from foam egg.

Fig. 1

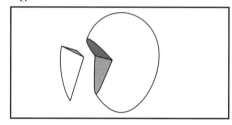

4. Use pattern to cut nose from cardboard. Pushing edge of cardboard into foam, glue nose 2" from narrow end of foam egg.

5. For chin, make a 1" dia. ball from foil; shape to form a chin. Use a straight pin to attach chin to foam egg.

6. Cut cuff from sock; set aside. Carefully pull sock over head. Gather edges of sock to back of head and glue to egg, trimming if necessary. Glue head to bottle lid.

7. For dress, tear a 13" x 25" piece of fabric. Fuse a length of web tape along one short edge on right side of fabric piece. Remove paper backing. Overlap short edges and fuse together, forming a tube. Baste along one edge of tube (top of dress). Place dress over bottle. Pull basting threads to gather dress tightly at neck; adjust gathers evenly. Knot thread and trim ends.

8. For sleeves, tear a 7" x 18" piece of fabric. Fuse a length of web tape along one long edge on right side of fabric. Remove paper backing. Overlap long edges and fuse together, forming a tube.

9. For arms, cut an 18" length of wire. Insert wire through sleeve tube. Use pattern to cut two hands from cardboard. Cover each cardboard hand with a 2¹/₂" square cut from cuff of sock; glue in place. Glue one hand to each end of wire arm. Turn sleeves under.

10. Gather sleeve tube at center; wrap with wire to secure. Glue center of arms to center back of dress at neck. Bend arms to front.

11. For cape, wrap an 11" x 16" piece of felt around body; secure at neck with a length of yarn tied into a bow.

12. For hair, glue lengths of raffia to head. Trim hair as desired; trim some hair for bangs.

13. Use pattern to cut four stars from poster board. Paint stars yellow.

14. For hatband, fold fabric scrap in half lengthwise; glue to hat. Wrap an 18" length of wire around hat next to hatband; bend as desired. Glue three stars to wire.

15. For "Treats" bag, cut a 3"x 4" piece of cardboard. Use pen to write "Treats" and draw stitches on cardboard. Glue remaining star to cardboard. Glue ends of a 5¹/₂" length of jute to back of cardboard for handle. Place handle over one hand; glue in place.

16. For broom, glue several 3¹/₂" lengths of raffia around end of twig. Wrap and knot a length of raffia around twig and broom bristles. Glue broom to hand.

17. Glue wiggle eyes to head. For mouth, bend a 2" length of wire into a "V" shape. Insert ends of wire through sock into foam between nose and chin. For tooth, cut a small rectangle of white paper. Glue tooth under mouth.

GHOULISH GOODY BUCKETS

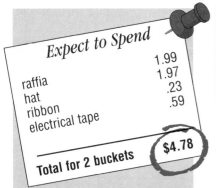

WHAT TO BUY

Orange raffia (2-oz. bag)
5" dia. black felt witch's hat
1/3 yd 3/8"w orange grosgrain
    ribbon
Black electrical tape

THINGS YOU HAVE AT HOME

White poster board, tracing paper,
transfer paper, stylus, colored
pencils, black felt-tip pen, one
2-liter and two 3-liter green soft
drink bottles, black thread, two
large buttons, large needle, and
glue

TECHNIQUES YOU'LL NEED

Making Patterns (pg. 104)

*R*ecycle your green soda bottles
into unique goody buckets at a cost
guaranteed to make any witch cackle
— two buckets for less than $5! These
kid-pleasing candy carriers are so
simple to cut, color, and paste that
you can stir up a caldronful of eerie
containers in no time!

WITCH TREAT BUCKETS

1. Transfer witch's face and hair patterns
(pg. 114) to poster board.

2. Use pencils to color face and hair. Use
pen to draw over transferred lines.

3. Glue strands of raffia over poster board
hair.

4. (**Note:** Cut hat in half; use 1/2 of hat for
each bucket.) Overlapping ends at back,
glue a 6" length of ribbon to hat half for
hatband. Tie several strands of raffia into a
bow. Glue bow and a button to hat. Glue hat
to top of witch's head.

5. (**Note:** Our bucket measures 9"h from
bottom to rim.) For bucket, cut top from
one 3-liter bottle. Cover cut edge of bottle
with electrical tape.

6. For handle, cut a 3/4" x 13 1/2" strip from
2-liter bottle. Wrap strip with electrical
tape. Use a needle and thread to fasten
ends of handle to bucket.

7. Glue witch to front of bucket.

HAPPY HALLOWEEN TABLE RUNNER

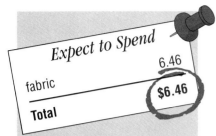

WHAT TO BUY

Fabric: 45"w
  5/8 yd muslin
  1/3 yd orange print for border
    and candy corn bottoms
  1/8 yd solid orange for candy
    corn
  1/8 yd each green and
    dark green for leaves
  1/8 yd light orange for small
    pumpkin
  1/4 yd each orange and
    dark orange for medium
    and large pumpkin
  1/8 yd black for faces
  1/8 yd brown for stems

THINGS YOU HAVE AT HOME

Paper-backed fusible web, white acrylic paint, paintbrush, and pressing cloth

TECHNIQUES YOU'LL NEED

Fusing Basics (pg. 104)
Painting Tips (pg. 105)

For less than $7, you can top your harvest table with jolly jack-o'-lanterns fresh from the pumpkin patch. This no-sew appliqué table runner comes together in a flash — thanks to fusible web!

TABLE RUNNER
Finished size: 18" x 44"
1. Cut an 18" x 44" piece of muslin for runner. Cut a 1½" x 24" piece from one long edge of border fabric for candy corn appliqués. Fuse web to remainder of border fabric. Cut two 3" x 44" strips and two 3" x 18" strips for border. Do not remove paper backing.

2. Use patterns (pgs. 117 and 118) to make appliqués from fabrics.

3. Paint tips of candy corn appliqués white.

4. Arrange appliqués on each end of runner; using pressing cloth over candy corn appliqués, fuse appliqués in place.

5. Press border strips in half lengthwise. Remove paper backing. Insert one long edge of muslin into one long border strip; fuse in place. Repeat for remaining long edge, then short edges of runner.

"Boo-gie" T-Shirt

WHAT TO BUY

One orange T-shirt (large enough
for a 15" x 20" design)
White acrylic paint
¹/₈ yd fabric for appliqués
¹/₂ yd ⁷/₈"w ribbon

THINGS YOU HAVE AT HOME

T-shirt form or cardboard covered
with waxed paper, tracing paper,
transfer paper, stylus, black
acrylic paint, paintbrushes, black
permanent felt-tip pen,
compressed craft sponges, paper-
backed fusible web, tear-away
stabilizer, black sewing thread,
and a small safety pin

TECHNIQUES YOU'LL NEED

Making Patterns (pg. 104)
Fusing Basics (pg. 104)
Painting Tips (pg. 105)
Stitched Appliqués (pg. 105)

*This not-so-scary skeleton is ready
to shake a leg at the Annual Goblin
Sock Hop! You can have a ghostly good
time transforming a bright orange tee
into this Halloween funwear. Getting
our boogie-woogie bag of bones to kick
up his heels is a snap with easy-to-
follow directions for sponge painting
and appliqué.*

SKELETON T-SHIRT

1. Wash and dry shirt without using fabric
softener; press.

2. Place shirt on T-shirt form.

3. Transfer skull pattern (pg. 70) to shirt,
allowing at least 20" between top of skull
and hem of shirt to accommodate design.

4. Basecoat skull white. Paint eyes and
nose black. Paint white highlights in eyes.
Use pen to draw mouth and cracks in skull.

5. Use tracing paper to make patterns for
bones (pg. 70). Use patterns to cut shapes
from sponges.

6. For skeleton body, use sponge shapes to
paint white bones on shirt.

7. Use patterns (pg. 117) to make
appliqués to spell "BOO!" Fuse appliqués to
shirt. Stitch appliqués in place.

8. Tie ribbon into a bow. Use safety pin on
wrong side of shirt to pin bow to shirt.

BEWITCHING BAGS

WHAT TO BUY

Five 6" x 9" purple gift bags
Five black felt pieces

THINGS YOU HAVE AT HOME

White poster board, tracing paper, transfer paper, stylus, colored pencils, black felt-tip pen, natural raffia, rubber bands, glue, and a chalk pencil

TECHNIQUES YOU'LL NEED

Making Patterns (pg. 104)

Our spellbinding bag is a real treat, especially when you can make five for only $2! Pack our wondrous witch with yummy delights for fabulous party favors. She's put together with super-simple patterns and a little bit of felt and raffia.

BEWITCHING BAGS

1. Transfer witch's face only and patches patterns (pg. 114) to poster board.

2. Use pencils to color face and patches. Use pen to draw over transferred lines and to draw stitches on patches. Cut out shapes.

(Continued on page 71)

SCARY PHOTO ALBUM
(Continued from page 58)

4. Cut a piece of orange fabric 8" x 9½"; fuse web to wrong side. Fuse web to wrong side of black fabric piece. Do not remove paper backing.

5. Use skull pattern (this page) to make appliqué from white fabric.

6. Fuse skull appliqué to center of right side of black fabric piece. Remove paper backing from black fabric piece and fuse to center of orange fabric piece. Transfer eyes and nose to skull. Paint eyes and nose black. Paint white highlights in eyes. Use pen to draw mouth and cracks in skull.

7. Fuse web tape to wrong side of ribbon length. Cut two 5" and two 6½" lengths of ribbon. Fuse ribbon lengths along edges of black fabric. Transfer words (pg. 71) to orange fabric. Use pen to draw over transferred words. Remove paper backing from orange fabric; center and fuse to album front.

8. Glue rickrack along edges of orange fabric. Glue buttons to corners of rickrack.

9. Tie several lengths of raffia into a bow and glue to album.

PUMPKIN-PATCH PULLOVER
(Continued from page 61)

4. Use three strands of orange floss to work Blanket Stitch along neck, bottom, and sleeve edges of sweatshirt.

5. Use pumpkin, stem, and leaf patterns (pgs. 117 and 118) to make appliqués from fabrics. Arrange appliqués on sweatshirt and fuse in place.

6. Use three strands of coordinating floss to work Blanket Stitch along edges of appliqués.

7. Use three strands of green floss to work Running Stitch for tendrils and vines between leaf and pumpkin appliqués on shoulder and sleeve; work French Knots at ends of tendrils.

8. Refer to **Fig. 1** to make a 1¼" pleat in sleeve; sew a button over pleat.

Fig. 1

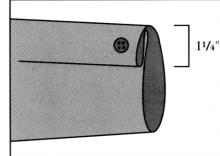

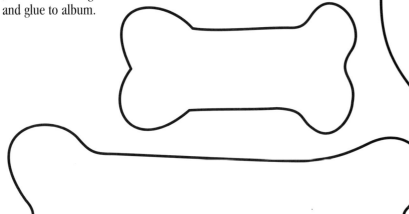

BONY SKELETON
(Continued from page 62)

3. For skeleton body, cut the following lengths from chenille stems: one 13" length for backbone, one 14" length for arms, one 17" length for legs, and three 5½" lengths for ribs.

4. (**Note:** Refer to **Diagram** for Steps 4 - 6.) For hanger, make a 2" long loop at end of backbone chenille stem; twist end to secure. For skeleton frame, wrap centers of chenille stems for arms, ribs, and legs around backbone; glue to secure.

5. Arrange bones and skull right side down. Glue end of torso bone to pelvic bone. Leave space between remaining bones. Place skeleton frame over bones and skull and glue in place.

6. To stabilize skeleton, cut one 5" and two 1¾" lengths of wire. Glue 5" wire length across shoulder and neck bones and 1¾" lengths in a "V" connecting torso to pelvic bones.

7. Tie ribbon into a bow around skeleton's neck.

DIAGRAM

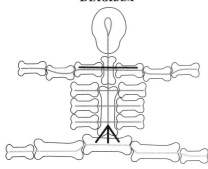

GOBLIN DOOR HANGER
(Continued from page 63)

6. Tie a 3" x 44" fabric strip into a bow around neck.

7. Use tracing paper to make leaf pattern (pg. 115). Cut three leaves from green foam. Cut a ¼" x 14" strip of green foam, tapering foam strip at ends. Wrap and glue around pumpkin stem. Glue one leaf to stem; glue two leaves below bow.

8. For banner, punch holes in corners of one long edge of a 7½" x 9" piece of yellow craft foam. Cut out photocopy of sign along circle. Glue sign to poster board; cut out sign. Use tracing paper to make "no" pattern (pg. 116). Cut shape from red felt. Glue felt shape to poster board sign. Glue sign to center of yellow craft foam piece. Insert a 27" length of ribbon through each hole in banner. Glue ribbons to ends of arms. Glue one button to each end of arms over ribbon.

BEWITCHING BAGS
(Continued from page 69)

3. Place treat in bag. Gather top of bag and secure with rubber band.

4. Glue face and patches to front of bag.

5. For hair, glue strands of raffia to top of head; cut hair to desired length.

6. For hat, make patterns (pg. 116). Use cone and large circle patterns to cut shapes from felt. Use chalk pencil to draw around small circle pattern at center of felt circle. Cutting into center of drawn circle, cut center of circle into wedges like a pie (**Fig. 1**).

Fig. 1

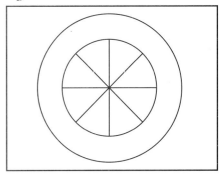

7. Overlap and glue straight edges of cone shape together to form top of hat. Fold and glue wedge sections of felt circle to inside of hat. Bend tip of hat down and glue to secure. Knot a length of raffia around hat for hatband.

8. Glue hat to top of head.

CAUTION: SCARY PHOTOS INSIDE!!

THANKSGIVING

*he spicy aroma of fresh-baked pumpkin pie and the chatter
of family and friends fill the air. It's Thanksgiving, a time for
feasting and fun, and a time to stop and reflect upon the blessings
in life. Aside from good health and a comfortable home, there is
a wealth of little things that are sometimes overlooked — like the joy
of creating. We have a cornucopia of projects that invites the
savoring of small pleasures. Color your home in shades of autumn
with our beautiful accent pieces while making Thanksgiving dinner
even more appetizing with festive table decorations — all fruits
of your own crafting. And since all the designs are fashioned from
inexpensive materials, you can count an extra blessing this season!*

*Add a natural centerpiece to
your Thanksgiving table for less
than $10! With the chilly autumn
wind whispering outside your
windows, our charming tree is
sure to warm your heart and
home. Rustic scarecrows, bows,
and miniature wreaths hang
handsomely from this affordable
tree, and a scattering of fall leaves
stylishly circles the base. (See pages
80 and 82 for instructions.)*

TURKEY NAPKIN HOLDERS

Expect to Spend

fabric	1.90
felt	1.98
ribbon	1.50
napkins	1.47
Total for 12 napkin holders	**$6.85**

WHAT TO BUY

¹/₂ yd orange fabric
¹/₂ yd 72"w ecru felt
Black felt piece
Three coordinating colors of
ribbon (10-yd spools)
9⁷/₈" square paper napkins

THINGS YOU
HAVE AT HOME

Paper-backed fusible web; white
poster board; white, yellow, and
red fabric scraps for appliqués;
white and yellow acrylic paint;
paintbrushes; black felt-tip pen;
and glue

TECHNIQUES
YOU'LL NEED

Fusing Basics (pg. 104)
Painting Tips (pg. 105)

Your Thanksgiving guests will enjoy an extra helping of fun with our Pilgrim turkey napkin holders! Easily made from poster board and felt with fanfolded napkin plumes, these cheerful accents welcome all to the feast. Since you can make 12 for less than $7, you'll have even more to be thankful for!

TURKEY NAPKIN HOLDERS

1. Cut one 18" x 24" piece each of poster board, ecru felt, and web. Use web to fuse felt to poster board.

2. Use patterns (pg. 120) to make twelve turkey head appliqués from orange fabric, twelve hat appliqués from black felt, and twelve each of hatband, beak, and wattle appliqués from scrap fabrics.

3. Arrange each group of turkey head, hat, hatband, beak, and wattle appliqués on felt side of posterboard, overlapping as necessary. Fuse in place and cut out.

4. Paint yellow buckles on hats. Use pen to draw eyes and eyelashes on turkeys and to outline buckles. Use white paint to highlight eyes.

5. For each napkin holder, cut a 27" length from each color ribbon. Glue centers of ribbons to back of turkey head 3" from bottom edge.

6. Unfold one napkin once and fanfold lengthwise. Matching ends, fold napkin in half. Tie ribbons into a bow around napkin. Repeat for each napkin holder.

PUMPKIN TURKEY

WHAT TO BUY

¹/₈ yd gold fabric
¹/₄ yd each of orange fabric and muslin
Three ecru felt pieces
Package of 10" long wooden skewers
White dimensional paint
Medium size pumpkin (we used a 10" dia. pumpkin)
7" dia. grapevine wreath

THINGS YOU HAVE AT HOME

Paper-backed fusible web, poster board, glue, fabric scraps for appliqués, white and yellow acrylic paint, paintbrushes, and black felt-tip pen

TECHNIQUES YOU'LL NEED

Fusing Basics (pg. 104)
Painting Tips (pg. 105)

*O*ur jolly Tom Turkey is a delightful way to decorate your dinner table! With a plump pumpkin body and appliqué feathers supported by wooden skewers, this colorful bird perches atop a grapevine wreath "nest." This festive centerpiece will liven up any meal!

TURKEY CENTERPIECE

1. Use patterns (pgs. 120 and 121) to make nine feather top appliqués from gold fabric, one turkey head and nine feather bottom appliqués from orange fabric, and nine whole feather appliqués from muslin. Make one each of hat, hatband, beak, and wattle appliqués from scrap fabrics.

2. Arrange feather tops and bottoms on felt, overlapping each top and bottom ¹/₈"; fuse in place. Cut feathers from felt.

3. Center and glue one skewer to felt side of each feather with pointed end of skewer extending 4" below bottom of feather.

4. Fuse one whole feather appliqué to back of each feather over skewer.

5. Cut one 4¹/₂" x 8" rectangle each from poster board, web, and felt; fuse felt rectangle to poster board rectangle. Arrange turkey head, hat, hatband, beak, and wattle appliqués on felt side of rectangle, overlapping as necessary. Fuse in place and cut out.

6. Use dimensional paint to paint over raw edges between feather top and bottom pieces. Paint buckle on hat yellow. Use pen to draw eyes and eyelashes on turkey and to outline buckle. Use white paint to highlight eyes.

7. Trim stem of pumpkin flat; glue turkey head to stem. Insert skewers of feathers into pumpkin. Place turkey on wreath.

HARVEST ANGEL

WHAT TO BUY

3¹/₂" long wooden Shaker peg
1¹/₂" dia. wooden bead for head
¹/₃ yd fabric
Ecru, gold, orange, and green
   felt pieces
Brown embroidery floss
Package (90 cu. in.) natural wood
   wool excelsior
Moss bird nest (2¹/₂" dia.)
Package of two 1¹/₂" dia.
   decorative pumpkins
Small autumn silk flowers

THINGS YOU HAVE AT HOME

Empty toilet tissue roll, drawing
compass, craft knife, cutting mat,
thread to match fabric and felt,
embroidery needle, tracing paper,
dressmaker's tracing paper, stylus,
black permanent felt-tip pen,
floral wire, wire cutters, lipstick,
buttons, and glue

TECHNIQUES YOU'LL NEED

Making Patterns (pg. 104)
Embroidery Stitches (pg. 106)
   Blanket Stitch
   Backstitch

The Thanksgiving Angel has arrived bearing fruits from the harvest! With a bird nest hat and quaint country clothing, this sweet-faced spirit is divinely affordable. An enchanting figure with her felt wings and golden hair, she offers bushels of blessings to all!

HARVEST ANGEL

1. To make shoulders, cut empty toilet tissue roll in half lengthwise; cut a 2¹/₂" length from one piece. Use compass to draw a ¹/₂" dia. circle at center of shoulders. Use craft knife to cut circle into wedges like a pie (**Fig. 1**). Insert Shaker peg through hole in shoulders.

Fig. 1

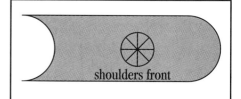

shoulders front

2. For torso and head, insert end of peg (neck) into bead (head) and glue in place.

3. For dress, cut a 12" x 16" fabric piece. Matching right sides and raw edges, use a ¹/₄" seam allowance to sew short edges together, forming a tube; turn right side out. Baste along one raw edge of dress. Place dress over torso and pull basting

(Continued on page 83)

AUTUMN APRON

WHAT TO BUY

Natural canvas apron
Fabric:
    1/4 yd each of gold and
        orange print for leaves
    1/8 yd brown print for leaves
    1/8 yd each of brown print
        and brown solid for
        acorns
Brown dimensional paint

THINGS YOU HAVE AT HOME

Paper-backed fusible web and a
T-shirt form

TECHNIQUES YOU'LL NEED

Fusing Basics (pg. 104)
Painting Tips (pg. 105)

*B*ake away on those cool
autumn days in our seasonal apron!
Richly colored leaf and acorn
appliqués drift lazily down the front
of the ready-made canvas apron and
create a soft, leafy border at the bottom.

AUTUMN APRON

1. Use patterns (pg. 120) to make six
maple leaf, four oak leaf, six acorn top, and
six acorn bottom appliqués.

2. Overlapping appliqués, arrange five
leaves 1/2" from lower edge across bottom
of apron. Arrange remaining leaves and
acorns on apron front. Fuse appliqués in
place.

3. Place T-shirt form under apron. Paint
over edges of leaves and acorns. Paint veins
and stems on leaves and tendrils on apron.

4. Cutting close to paint outline on leaf
shapes, carefully trim excess fabric from
bottom of apron.

NATURALLY BEAUTIFUL WREATH

Expect to Spend

fabric	1.61
floral pins	1.09
wreath	2.47
beads	1.49
corn husks	2.99
Total	**$9.65**

WHAT TO BUY

¹/₈ yd each of five coordinating
    fabrics
Floral pins (60 count)
16" dia. straw wreath
12mm wooden beads (12 pack)
4-oz. package of corn husks

THINGS YOU
HAVE AT HOME

Brown paper bags, natural raffia,
glue, floral wire, wire cutters,
plastic bag, and paper towels

*B*ring *a natural touch to your
decor with our beautiful fall wreath!
Fashioned from bunched squares
of brown paper and fabric, the
ring is highlighted with an array of
corn-husk flowers and a rich russet
bow. Whether it's hanging inside or
on the front door, the piece offers
a stunning welcome!*

AUTUMN WREATH

1. For hanger, bend an 18" length of floral
wire in half. Twist wire together 2" from
bend to form a loop. Keeping loop at back
of wreath, wrap wire ends around wreath
and twist together to secure.

2. Fringe edges of one fabric piece and tie
into bow; set aside.

3. Cut or tear 3¹/₂" squares from paper
bags and fabrics, making 200 brown paper
squares and 40 fabric squares.

4. For each fabric/paper bunch, layer
one paper piece, one fabric piece (right
side up), then two paper pieces. Make
40 fabric/paper bunches. For each paper
bunch, layer four paper pieces. Make
20 paper bunches.

5. Push a floral pin through center of each
bunch. Arrange and pin bunches close
together, folding edges away from wreath to
create fullness and cover wreath.

6. (**Note:** Follow Steps 6 - 9 to make
twelve flowers.) For flowers, soak corn
husks in warm water for 40 minutes or
until pliable. To keep husks damp after

(Continued on page 83)

MAPLE LEAF COASTER SET

WHAT TO BUY

1/4 yd 72"w ecru felt
1/4 yd each of four coordinating fabrics
Small basket

THINGS YOU HAVE AT HOME

Paper-backed fusible web, tracing paper, jute twine, buttons, and glue

TECHNIQUES YOU'LL NEED

Making Patterns (pg. 104)
Fusing Basics (pg. 104)

Blend seasonal beauty and the comforts of home with our maple leaf coasters! Inexpensively crafted, the brilliant leaves and button-accented storage basket complement cozy autumn gatherings.

MAPLE LEAF COASTER SET

1. Cut felt into four 9" x 15" pieces. Fuse two pieces together; repeat with remaining two pieces.

2. Cut a 9" x 15" piece from each color fabric. Fuse web to wrong side of each fabric piece. Fuse one fabric piece to each side of each fused felt piece.

3. Use tracing paper to make maple leaf pattern (pg. 120). Use pattern to cut three shapes from each fabric-covered felt piece.

4. For each stem, cut a 5" length of jute and knot ends together. Twist and glue loop of jute and one button to each leaf.

5. Glue buttons along rim of basket.

THANKSGIVING BAGS

Expect to Spend

felt	1.60
embroidery floss	.20
wreaths	.99
flowers	1.19
jute twine	.99
Total for 4 bags	**$4.97**

WHAT TO BUY

Two pieces each of gold, orange, green, and brown felt
Brown embroidery floss
Four 4" dia. grapevine wreaths
Silk flowers
Jute twine (3-ply)

THINGS YOU HAVE AT HOME

Pinking shears, embroidery needle, drawing compass, brown paper bag, black felt-tip pen, and glue

TECHNIQUES YOU'LL NEED

Embroidery Stitches (pg. 106)
  Running Stitch

*S*urprise guests with nifty "Give Thanks" grab bags! Soft felt and jute twine bows make handsome packages for your gifts. With tiny rustic wreaths attached, these generous tokens will be enjoyed as much as the treats inside!

"GIVE THANKS" BAGS

1. For each bag, layer two felt pieces and pin together. Use pinking shears to trim ¼" from edges of felt pieces.

2. To make bag, use six strands of floss to work Running Stitch ¼" from side and bottom edges of layered felt pieces, leaving top of bag open.

3. Use compass to draw a 3¾" dia. circle on brown paper bag; cut out.

4. Use pen to write "Give Thanks" at center of paper circle. Center and glue paper circle to back of wreath.

5. Glue several flowers around wreath.

6. Place gift in bag.

7. Cut two 42" lengths of jute twine and thread through wreath, centering wreath on twine. With wreath at front of bag, wrap twine around top of bag twice to gather; tie into a bow.

WHEAT-HEART CANDLE HOLDER

Expect to Spend

wheat	2.99
ribbon	.65
candle holder	1.99
candle	1.99
clay saucer	.48
Total	**$8.10**

WHAT TO BUY

Natural golden wheat stalks
   (6-oz. package)
2/3 yd 1 3/4"w wire-edged ribbon
3 1/2" dia. x 7 1/2"h clear glass
   candle holder
3" dia. x 6"h pillar candle
4 1/2" dia. clay saucer

THINGS YOU
HAVE AT HOME

Cotton string and natural raffia

*B*ring *a harvest of love and prosperity to your home with our symbolic candle holder. Shaped into a heart, the golden stalks transform a simple glass sleeve into a naturally beautiful showpiece. A thoughtful gift, the project is an ideal way to express your appreciation during the traditional season of thanks!*

WHEAT CANDLE HOLDER

1. Soak fifteen wheat strands in water for 30 minutes.

2. With wheat heads even, use string to tie strands together near heads. Wrap and knot a length of raffia over string.

3. To braid wheat stalks, divide into three groups: four stalks to the left, seven stalks in the middle, and four stalks to the right. To braid each four-straw section, hold the section in your left hand (palm up) with wheat heads down and the four straws held securely between the first and second fingers at the point where they are tied. Bend the four straws to point them in north, south, east, and west positions. With your right hand, fold the north straw to the south, the south straw to the north, then the east straw to the west and the west straw to the east. Fold straws straight over; do not twist or change sides. Continue until each braid is 4" long.

4. Shape braided lengths into a heart, overlapping ends over the seven free stalks at center. Use string to tie cross section at top of heart to seven center stalks; trim

(Continued on page 83)

RUSTIC SCARECROW SWAG

Expect to Spend

fabric	1.04
beads	1.29
hats	.39
felt	.40
ribbon	1.96
silk leaves	1.19
Total	**$6.27**

WHAT TO BUY

¹/₈ yd each:
  gold fabric for shirt
  orange fabric for shirt
  brown fabric for pants
25mm wooden beads (4 pack)
Three 2¹/₄" dia. straw hats
Gold and orange felt pieces
1¹/₂"w natural fiber ribbon
  (8-yd spool)
Autumn silk leaves

THINGS YOU HAVE AT HOME

Natural raffia, rubber bands,
tracing paper, pinking shears,
glue, floral wire, wire cutters, and
acorns

TECHNIQUES YOU'LL NEED

Making Patterns (pg. 104)

*R*esembling a string of rustic
farm boys with their ragtag clothes
and straw hats, these raffia figures
stand watch among a smattering of
silk autumn leaves. This thrifty
scarecrow swag will bring the down-
home feel of a country harvest to
your mantel.

SCARECROW SWAG

1. For each scarecrow, cut several strands
of raffia 7¹/₂" long to make a bundle for
body and legs. Use a rubber band to hold
bundle together close to one end (neck).
Cut 20 - 25 strands of raffia 6" long to
make bundle for arms. To attach arms, cut
three 6" strands of raffia. Center arms
across body ¹/₂" below neck end. Tie 6"
raffia strands around arms and body in a
crisscross fashion. Knot in place. If
necessary, glue to secure.

2. Use tracing paper to make shirt and
pants patterns (pg. 119). Use patterns to
cut one shirt and two pants shapes from

fabrics; fold shirt in half. Use pinking
shears to trim edges of sleeves and bottom
edges of pant legs.

3. Place shirt over neck of scarecrow; glue
side and sleeve seams. Place pants pieces
on scarecrow front and back, overlapping
top of pants ¹/₄" over shirt; glue in place.
Divide raffia bundle in half for legs; glue
pants together along inseams and sides
around legs. Cut three 7" strands of raffia
and tie into a bow around waist; trim ends.

4. Remove rubber band from neck and
glue ¹/₂" of bundle into hole in bead. Glue
hat to top of head.

5. Repeat steps 1 - 4 to make a total of
three scarecrows.

6. For swag, use pinking shears to cut four
1¹/₄" x 11¹/₂" strips from gold felt and four
³/₄" x 11¹/₂" strips from orange felt. Center
orange strips over gold strips and glue in
place. Overlap ends of strips ³/₄" and glue
together.

(Continued on page 83)

82

HARVEST ANGEL
(Continued from page 76)

threads to gather dress. Knot and trim thread ends. Glue dress to body at neck. Fringe bottom of dress.

4. Use tracing paper to make jacket and wing patterns (pg. 119).

5. Use pattern to cut jacket from gold felt. Cut down center front of jacket. Use a $1/8$" seam allowance to sew side and sleeve seams of jacket. Use six strands of floss to work Blanket Stitch along all raw edges of jacket.

6. Transfer tendril pattern to front pieces of jacket. Use six strands of floss to work Backstitch over tendril design.

7. Use pattern (pg. 119) to cut two pumpkins from orange felt. Glue pumpkins to jacket front. Use pen to draw stitches on pumpkins. Use pattern (pg. 119) to cut two pumpkin stems from green felt; glue stems to pumpkins.

8. Place jacket over shoulders. For dress sleeves, cut a 3" x 12" fabric piece. Matching right sides and raw edges, use a $1/4$" seam allowance to sew long edges together, forming a tube; turn right side out. For arms, insert a 12" length of floral wire through sleeves. Glue sleeves to wire at ends. Bending wire slightly, insert arm piece through jacket sleeves and glue to each end of torso.

9. For bows, cut three $1/2$" x 1" pieces of green felt. Wrap a length of embroidery floss around center of each bow; knot and trim ends. Spacing evenly, glue bows to jacket front.

10. For face, use pen to draw eyes and nose. Use fingertip to apply lipstick to cheeks for blush.

11. Glue excelsior to head for hair; trim to desired length. Glue bird nest to head for hat. Glue one flower to hat.

12. Glue excelsior, pumpkins, and three flowers to arms. Glue buttons along bottom front of dress.

13. Use pattern to cut two wings from ecru felt; glue wings together. Use six strands of floss to work Blanket Stitch along edges of wings.

14. For hanger, cut a $1/2$" x $6^{1/2}$" strip of ecru felt. Fold strip in half to form a loop. Glue 1" of ends of loop to one side of wings; glue hanger side of wings to angel back.

NATURALLY BEAUTIFUL WREATH
(Continued from page 78)

soaking, place corn husks in a resealable plastic bag with a damp paper towel.

7. For flower center, cut a 6" length of floral wire and several 4" strands of raffia. Insert raffia through one bead; glue in place. Insert floral wire through bead and twist ends close to bead, leaving a 4" long tail.

8. (**Note:** Refer to **Figs. 1** and **2** for Step 8.) Pat a few pieces of corn husk dry between paper towels. Tear two $1^{1/2}$"w strips, one 3"w strip, and two 5"w strips for each flower. Holding the bead by wire stem in one hand, make a loop in one $1^{1/2}$"w strip and scrunch around base of bead, pinching tightly around wire stem. Repeat with remaining $1^{1/2}$"w strips, 3"w, then 5"w strips, fanning wider strips around narrow strips.

Fig. 1

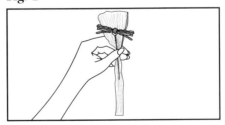

Fig. 2

9. Secure husks tightly at base of bead by wrapping with floral wire. Bring ends of 5"w strips up toward flower and trim to resemble leaves. Leaving $1/2$" of corn husks below wire, trim excess. Allow flower to dry completely.

10. Glue flowers to wreath between fabric and paper bunches.

11. Thread a 12" length of floral wire through back of bow knot and secure bow to bottom of wreath.

WHEAT-HEART CANDLE HOLDER
(Continued from page 81)

unbraided ends of stalks forming heart to $1/4$" long. Wrap and knot a length of raffia over string. Trim ends of seven free stalks to $1^{1/4}$" above heart.

5. Weight braided heart with a heavy object and allow to dry overnight.

6. Tie a 24" length of ribbon around candle holder; knot ribbon ends around wheat decoration. Cut a "V"-shaped notch in ribbon ends.

7. Place candle in holder. Glue holder to inverted saucer.

RUSTIC SCARECROW SWAG
(Continued from page 82)

7. Glue scarecrows over ends of swag strips.

8. For each ribbon bow, cut a 28" length of ribbon; form into a bow. Twist a 4" length of floral wire around bow center to secure. Glue an acorn to center of bow. Glue a bow to each end of swag.

9. For each raffia bow, cut five 26" strands of raffia; tie into a bow. Use another length of raffia to tie bow to swag between two scarecrows.

10. Glue silk leaves to swag.

CHRISTMAS

O *Christmastime, O Christmastime, O what a festive holiday
time! Carols and cards, parties and presents — the exciting press
of things to do and people to remember may leave you wishing
for your own jolly elf to manage matters! For a crafty answer to
the holiday's expanding gift lists and pinched pocketbooks, create
your own winter wonderland with our appealing homemade
projects. As you make these gifts, home decorations, and clothing
using easy-to-find, inexpensive materials, you can enjoy all the
pleasures of the season, from simple to sublime.*

*Trimmed with a cozy touch of
plaid, our colorful centerpiece tree
celebrates frosty weather at a
heartwarming price. You'll spend
less than $10 decorating it with a
sprinkling of charming felt mittens,
snowflakes, and snow buddies. An
old-fashioned popcorn garland adds
a taste of nostalgia.* (See pages 92
and 97 for instructions.)

WOODSY SNOW ANGEL

This woodsy snow angel is sure to bring wintry blessings to your home. A gold wire halo and stiffened flannel wings transform a traditional snowman, crafted of stuffed felt, into an angelic center of attention. What a playful touch for your table or mantel!

Expect to Spend

felt	1.66
flannel	1.14
pearl cotton thread	.97
embroidery floss	.20
buttons	.57
fiberfill	1.72
wire	2.67
Total	**$8.93**

WHAT TO BUY

1/4 yd 72"w ecru felt
1/8 yd 72"w green felt
One orange felt piece
1/4 yd plaid flannel
One skein ecru pearl cotton thread (size 5)
Black embroidery floss
Three 1/2" dia. black buttons
Polyester fiberfill (12-oz. bag)
20-gauge gold wire (10-yd spool)

THINGS YOU HAVE AT HOME

Tracing paper, paper-backed fusible web, removable fabric marking pen, pins, embroidery needle, cardboard, small sharp scissors, wire cutters, two 8" long twigs, and glue

TECHNIQUES YOU'LL NEED

Making Patterns (pg. 104)
Fusing Basics (pg. 104)
Embroidery Stitches (pg. 106)
    Satin Stitch
    Running Stitch
    French Knot
    Cross Stitch

SNOWMAN ANGEL

1. Use tracing paper to make snowman, nose, wing, and base patterns (pg. 126).

2. Use patterns to cut two snowmen from ecru felt and one nose from orange felt.

3. Fuse web to wrong side of flannel. Cut two 6¹/₂" x 15¹/₂" pieces from fused flannel and one 6¹/₂" x 15¹/₂" piece from ecru felt. Fuse one flannel piece to each side of felt piece. Use fabric marking pen to draw around wing pattern on one side of fused flannel. Cut out wings along drawn line.

4. For scarf, cut a 1¹/₂" x 24" strip of green felt. For fringe, make 1" clips in each end of felt.

5. Use six strands of floss to work Satin Stitch for eyes and three strands of floss to work Running Stitch and French Knots for mouth. Use pearl cotton thread to work Cross Stitches to attach edge of nose to snowman. Use floss to sew buttons to snowman front.

6. Overlap edges of front snowman piece ⁵/₈" over edges of back snowman piece; pin in place. Starting at bottom left edge and leaving bottom edge open, use pearl cotton thread to work Cross Stitches along edge of snowman to stitch pieces together. Stuff snowman with fiberfill. Baste along open lower edge. Pull threads to close opening slightly; knot thread ends together.

7. Use base pattern to cut shape from cardboard. Cut a piece of ecru felt ¹/₂" larger on all sides than cardboard base. Clip edges of felt base slightly and center cardboard on felt; glue edges of felt over edges of cardboard. Glue wrong side of base to bottom of snowman.

8. Pin center of scarf 6" from top on back of snowman. Center wings on snowman with top edge of wings ¹/₂" below top edge of scarf; pin in place. Use pearl cotton thread to work Cross Stitches down center of wings to attach wings and scarf to snowman. Loosely tie scarf at front of snowman.

9. Use sharp scissors to carefully cut a hole between two Cross Stitches on each side of snowman below scarf. Insert 2" of one twig into each hole and glue in place.

10. For halo, cut two 30" lengths of wire. Twist wires together to form a 4" dia. circle. Leaving a 3" stem of wire, twist ends to secure. Insert stem between layers at top of snowman.

FOLKSY FELT STOCKINGS

WHAT TO BUY

Tree and Cat Stocking:
1/4 yd each of red and black
   54"w felt
Green, tan, and brown felt pieces
   for appliqués
Ecru embroidery floss
Snowman and Dog Stocking:
1/4 yd each of red and black
   54"w felt
Ecru, red, tan, and brown felt
   pieces for appliqués
One skein each of ecru and grey
   embroidery floss

THINGS YOU HAVE AT HOME

Tracing paper, paper-backed
fusible web, tear-away stabilizer,
felt scrap for snowman nose
appliqué, black thread,
embroidery needle, buttons, and
pinking shears

TECHNIQUES YOU'LL NEED

Making Patterns (pg. 104)
Stitched Appliqués (pg. 105)
Embroidery Stitches (pg. 106)
   Straight Stitch
   Running Stitch
   Cross Stitch

*W*himsical pets add a folksy touch
to holiday stockings so economical that
each can be made for less than $3!
Designed to be loved season after season,
these lighthearted stockings have pinked
edges, appealing felt appliqués, jaunty
buttons, and stitched snowflakes.

TREE AND CAT STOCKING

1. Use tracing paper to make stocking
pattern (pg. 125). Use pattern to cut one
stocking front from black felt.

2. Use patterns (pg. 121) to make tree, cat,
and trunk appliqués from felt.

3. Arrange and fuse appliqués on stocking
front.

4. Use zigzag stitch and black thread to
machine stitch appliqués in place.

5. Use three strands of floss to work
Straight Stitches for snowflakes.

6. Use black thread to work Straight
Stitches for whiskers and eyes on cat.

7. Sew buttons to stocking front.

8. Place stocking front on red felt piece.
Leaving top edge unstitched, use a zigzag
stitch and black thread to machine stitch
edges of stocking front to felt piece.

9. Use pinking shears to trim stocking back
to 1/2" from edges of stocking front.

10. For hanger, cut a 1 1/2" x 5 1/2" piece of
felt. Fold felt piece in half lengthwise. Use a
zigzag stitch to sew long edges together.
Fold hanger in half to form a loop. Tack
ends of hanger to top back of stocking. Sew
button to front of stocking over ends of
hanger.

(Continued on page 102)

RUSTIC COASTER SET

Expect to Spend

Shaker box	1.49
paint	1.98
crackle medium	1.27
felt	.60
buttons	.57
embroidery floss	.20
Total for coaster set	**$6.11**

WHAT TO BUY

4¹/₂" dia. Shaker box
Burgundy and green acrylic paint
2-oz. bottle crackle medium
Burgundy, green, and black felt
  pieces
Three ¹/₂" dia. buttons
Ecru embroidery floss

THINGS YOU HAVE AT HOME

Tracing paper, paintbrushes,
paper-backed fusible web, tear-
away stabilizer, black permanent
felt-tip pen, white acrylic paint,
matte acrylic spray sealer, pinking
shears, embroidery needle, black
thread, and glue

TECHNIQUES YOU'LL NEED

Making Patterns (pg. 104)
Fusing Basics (pg. 104)
Stitched Appliqués (pg. 105)
Painting Tips (pg. 105)
Embroidery Stitches (pg. 106)
  Straight Stitch

*T*hese rustic felt coasters — complete with a wooden storage box — offer a warm way to say "thank you" to any homemaker on your gift list. Crackle medium gives the painted box a distinctive finish that will last through many seasons of treasure-keeping.

TREE COASTERS AND BOX

1. Use tracing paper to make tree pattern (pg. 122).

2. Follow manufacturers' instructions to apply paint and crackle medium to box.

3. Draw around tree pattern on lid. Paint tree green. Paint white snowflakes on lid.

Use pen to draw cross stitches along edges of tree. Spray box with sealer.

4. Glue buttons to lid.

5. Use patterns (pg. 122) to make tree appliqués from green felt and circle appliqués from black felt. Do not remove paper backing from circles.

6. For each coaster, fuse one tree to one circle. Use three strands of embroidery floss to work Straight Stitches for snowflakes. Fuse black circle to burgundy felt. Leaving a ¹/₄" burgundy border, use pinking shears to cut around coaster.

7. Use a zigzag stitch and black thread to machine stitch appliqués in place.

ELEGANT MOSAIC BALLS

UNDER $5!

WHAT TO BUY

Four 4" dia. plastic foam balls
 (2 packs of 2)
8-oz. container Aleene's Designer
 Tacky Glue™
15" x 20" cold-press illustration
 board (2 pack)
Ceramcoat® Napthol Crimson
 (02408), Aleene's Gold™
 (0C301), Aleene's Holiday
 Green™, and black acrylic
 paint
One 16-oz. tub premixed
 spackling compound
1/4"w red satin ribbon
 (10-yd spool)

THINGS YOU
HAVE AT HOME

Tracing paper, rotary cutter or
craft knife, cutting mat, ruler,
paintbrushes, black permanent
felt-tip pen, cup, craft sticks,
sponges, plastic bowl, straight
pins, and acrylic spray sealer

TECHNIQUES
YOU'LL NEED

Making Patterns (pg. 104)
Painting Tips (pg. 105)

*D*elight friends and family with this
exquisite mosaic poinsettia ornament.
The pretty design is created by gluing
pieces of painted illustration board onto
a foam ball. Tinted spackling finishes the
unique gilded decoration, which glitters
and gleams as it catches the light.

MOSAIC BALLS

1. Cut the following pieces from illustration
board: one 2" x 15" strip for green; one
5" x 15" strip for red; and one 13" x 15"
strip for metallic gold. Paint strips as
indicated. Spray each painted strip with
sealer.

2. (**Note:** When cutting mosaic pieces, you
can use scissors, rotary cutter, or craft
knife. To give your design a handmade
look, cut pieces in varying shapes and
sizes. When gluing pieces to ball, leave about 1/16"
between pieces.) For mosaic pieces, cut
painted strips into approx. 5/8"w strips. Cut
strips into irregularly shaped triangle and
rectangle pieces.

3. (**Note:** Pattern only indicates shape of
flower, not size of mosaic pieces. There are
six flowers on each ball.) Use tracing paper
to make six poinsettia patterns (pg. 122).

4. Beginning at top and bottom of ball,
arrange patterns and pin to ball. Use pen to
draw around patterns on ball. Remove
pattern pieces.

5. (**Note:** To stabilize ball, place ball in
cup while working. Working from center of
each flower out, complete all of the flower
centers, petals, and leaves before filling in
between flowers.) Working on one small
area at a time and coating area completely,
use craft stick to spread glue on ball; press
mosaic pieces into glue, using gold pieces
for flower centers, red pieces for flower
petals, and green pieces between petals for
leaves. Fill in remaining areas with gold
mosaic pieces. Allow glue to dry overnight.
Apply sealer to ball.

(Continued on page 102)

PLAID FOREST TREE SKIRT

WHAT TO BUY

1½ yds 54"w burgundy felt
Three tan felt pieces
½ yd plaid flannel
¼ yd each of three green fabrics
for tree appliqués
Tan embroidery floss

THINGS YOU HAVE AT HOME

String, chalk pencil, thumbtack, clear nylon thread, thread to match felt for tree skirt, brown fabric scraps for tree trunk appliqués, paper-backed fusible web, tear-away stabilizer, buttons, and embroidery needle

TECHNIQUES YOU'LL NEED

Fusing Basics (pg. 104)
Stitched Appliqués (pg. 105)
Embroidery Stitches (pg. 106)
 Straight Stitch

*H*eighten the magic under your Christmas tree with our easy-to-make felt tree skirt. Plaid flannel trim, embroidered snowflakes, and button-embellished trees are charming touches.

APPLIQUÉD TREE SKIRT

1. Fold burgundy felt in half from top to bottom and again from left to right.

2. Tie one end of string to chalk pencil. Insert thumbtack through string 26" from pencil. Insert thumbtack in fabric, as shown in **Fig. 1**, to mark outer cutting line. Insert thumbtack through string 2" from pencil and repeat to mark inner cutting line.

Fig. 1

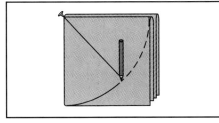

3. Cut along marked lines through all layers of felt. For opening at back, cut through one layer of felt from outer to inner edge.

4. For border, cut a 1½" x 4²/₃-yd bias strip from flannel, piecing as necessary. Pin bias strip 2" from outer edge of tree skirt. Trim ends of strip even with edges of tree

(Continued on page 102)

91

SIMPLE GIFT BAGS

You can turn simple materials into charming packages — at a fraction of the cost of purchased gift bags! Plaid ribbon, jolly red mittens, and perky buttons and bells jazz up everyday brown lunch bags, keeping holiday delights hidden from curious eyes.

TALL BAG (A)

1. Follow **Mittens** instructions to make one pair of mittens. Glue mittens to bag. Glue buttons to bag.

2. Line bag with tissue paper.

BAG WITH CUFF (B)

1. For cuff, fold top of bag down 1"; repeat. Use pen to draw stitches on cuff.

2. Follow **Mittens** instructions to make one pair of mittens. Glue mittens to bag. Glue buttons to bag.

3. Line bag with fabric scrap.

BAG WITH FLAP (C)

1. Fuse web to wrong side of a 5" x 6" fabric piece. Fuse fabric to top back of bag. Place gift in bag. For flap, fold top corners diagonally to front of bag forming a point; glue in place.

2. Use tracing paper to make small border pattern (this page). Use pattern to cut two borders from ecru felt. Glue edges of borders to underside of flap. Fold flap to front of bag and staple at center. Glue button over staple.

3. Follow **Mittens** instructions to make one pair of mittens. Wrap yarn connecting mittens around button.

Mittens

1. Use tracing paper to make small mitten and cuff patterns (pg. 124).

2. Use patterns to cut four mittens from red felt and two cuffs from ecru felt.

3. Use pearl cotton thread to work Straight Stitches and French Knots for snowflakes on two mitten shapes.

4. Gluing ends of a 10" yarn length between shapes, glue remaining mitten shapes to backs of mitten fronts. Glue cuffs to mittens.

BAG WITH BELL (D)

1. Use tracing paper to make large border pattern (this page). Use pattern to cut one border from ecru felt.

2. Place gift in bag.

3. For flap, fold top of bag ½" to front; fold 2½" to front again. Glue straight edge of border to under side of flap. Use pen to draw stitches on flap. Staple bag closed at center of flap.

4. Tear a 1½" x 20" piece of flannel. Thread flannel piece through hanger of bell and tie into a bow. Glue bow to bag over staple.

WHAT TO BUY

Brown lunch bags (50 pack)
One ecru and two red felt pieces
One skein ecru pearl cotton thread (size 5)
One skein red yarn (3 oz.)
¼ yd fabric for bag with flap
⅛ yd plaid flannel
One package 35mm jingle bells (2 pack)

THINGS YOU HAVE AT HOME

Tracing paper, embroidery needle, glue, tissue paper, black felt-tip pen, fabric scrap, buttons, paper-backed fusible web, and stapler

TECHNIQUES YOU'LL NEED

Making Patterns (pg. 104)
Fusing Basics (pg. 104)
Embroidery Stitches (pg. 106)
    Straight Stitch
    French Knot

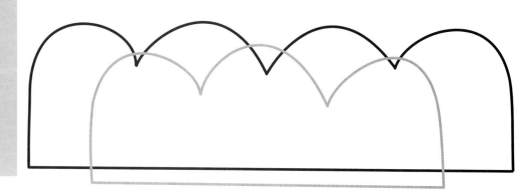

Charming Little Vest

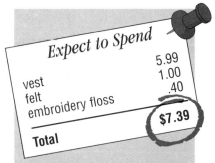
WHAT TO BUY

Child-size felt vest
Five felt pieces for appliqués (we used yellow, bright pink, red, green, and purple)
Two skeins embroidery floss (we used red)

THINGS YOU HAVE AT HOME

Tracing paper, paper-backed fusible web, pinking shears, embroidery needle, black permanent felt-tip pen, and buttons

TECHNIQUES YOU'LL NEED

Fusing Basics (pg. 104)
Embroidery Stitches (pg. 106)
    Running Stitch
    Cross Stitch
    Backstitch

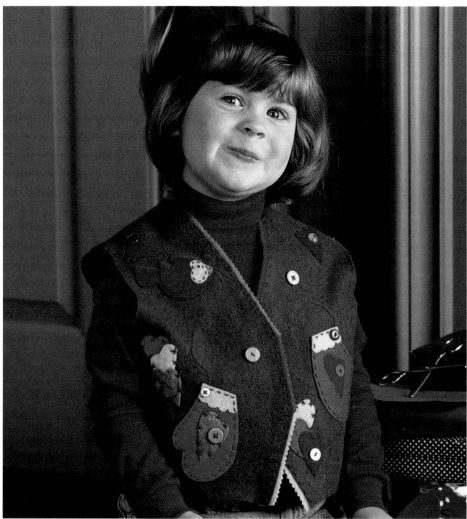

A playful redbird chases winter chills away as it flits across this snuggly topper crafted from a readymade felt vest. The bright colors of the appliqués are repeated in the whimsical buttons, border, and simple stitchery.

CHILD'S VEST

1. Use patterns (pg. 124) to make small mitten, cuff, bird, and heart appliqués from felt.

2. Arrange and fuse appliqués on vest.

3. For border strips, use pinking shears to cut ³/₄"w strips of felt. Overlapping ends and trimming to fit, pin strips to wrong side of vest front and neck edges. To attach strips to vest, use six strands of floss to work Running Stitch along edges of vest.

4. On appliqués, use six strands of floss to work Running Stitch along outer edges of cuffs, mittens, and birds and Cross Stitches along edges of hearts. Work Backstitch for string between mittens and birds.

5. Use pen to draw eye on bird. Use floss to sew buttons to vest.

COZY HOLIDAY SHIRT

WHAT TO BUY

Adult-size sweatshirt
Five felt pieces for appliqués (we
  used yellow, bright pink, red,
  green, and purple)
Three skeins embroidery floss
  (we used red)

**THINGS YOU
HAVE AT HOME**

Tracing paper, paper-backed
fusible web, embroidery needle,
black permanent felt-tip pen, and
buttons

**TECHNIQUES
YOU'LL NEED**

Fusing Basics (pg. 104)
Embroidery Stitches (pg. 106)
  Blanket Stitch
  Running Stitch
  Cross Stitch
  Backstitch

*Spread holiday fun with this cheery
pullover created from an inexpensive
plain sweatshirt. The felt appliqués are
embellished with blanket stitching and
buttons. You'll enjoy this cozy top all
winter long.*

APPLIQUÉD SWEATSHIRT

1. Use patterns (pg. 124) to make large
mitten, cuff, bird, and heart appliqués from
felt.

2. Arrange and fuse appliqués on
sweatshirt.

3. Use six strands of floss to work Blanket
Stitch along outer edges of cuff and mitten
appliqués, Running Stitch along edges of
bird appliqués, and Cross Stitch along
edges of heart appliqués. Work Backstitch
for string between mittens and birds.

4. Use pen to draw eyes on birds. Use floss
to sew buttons to sweatshirt.

JOLLY SNOWMAN ORNAMENTS

WHAT TO BUY

Four 4" dia. plastic foam balls
  (2 packs of 2)
One 4-oz. jar of artificial textured
  snow
Orange and red felt pieces

THINGS YOU
HAVE AT HOME

Paintbrushes, nail, drawing
compass, paper, poster board,
four small cans for hats (we used
3-oz. cat food cans), thumbtack,
black acrylic paint, twenty-eight
approx. ½" dia. pebbles, craft
knife, cutting mat, clear nylon
thread, and glue

TECHNIQUES
YOU'LL NEED

Painting Tips (pg. 105)

Bestow a frosty touch on your Christmas tree with a jolly snowman painted with artificial snow. This cute fellow has a tin can hat, an orange felt nose, and eyes made of painted pebbles! You can make four ornaments from foam balls for less than $7, so plan on sharing them with friends.

SNOWMAN ORNAMENTS

1. Paint each foam ball with a thin layer of artificial snow. (For ease in handling, place foam ball on nail for painting.)

2. For each hat, use compass to draw a 4" dia. circle pattern. Use pattern to cut hat brim from poster board.

3. Center open end of can on poster board circle; draw around can. Use craft knife to cut drawn circle into wedges like a pie (**Fig. 1**). Fold each wedge-shaped section to inside of can and glue in place.

Fig. 1

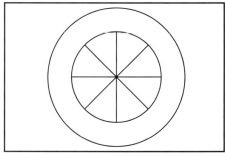

(Continued on page 102)

EASY WINTER WREATH

Expect to Spend

felt	2.75
wreath form	4.49
embroidery floss	.20
flannel	.57
pearl cotton thread	.97
Total	**$8.98**

WHAT TO BUY

$1/2$ yd 72"w green felt
One orange and three ecru felt
   pieces
14" dia. smooth foam wreath form
Black embroidery floss
$1/8$ yd plaid flannel
One skein ecru pearl cotton
   thread (size 5)

THINGS YOU
HAVE AT HOME

Green sewing thread, pinking
shears, serrated knife, tracing
paper, polyester fiberfill,
removable fabric marking pen,
small sharp scissors, large button,
embroidery needle, floral wire,
wire cutters, and glue

TECHNIQUES
YOU'LL NEED

Making Patterns (pg. 104)
Embroidery Stitches (pg. 106)
   Satin Stitch
   Running Stitch
   Straight Stitch
   French Knot

A cozy plaid bow sets off the rich green of our easy-to-assemble felt wreath. The endearing charm and very reasonable cost of this crafty decoration make it especially impressive.

FELT WREATH

1. For wreath, use pinking shears to cut four $8^{1}/_{2}$" x 35" strips from green felt. Using a $1^{1}/_{2}$" seam allowance, sew long edges of two strips together to form a tube. Repeat with remaining strips.

2. Use knife to cut a 2" section from wreath form. Thread felt tubes onto wreath. Replace 2" section and glue to secure. Adjust felt tubes evenly around wreath.

3. For hanger, wrap a 24" length of wire around top of wreath at gap between felt tubes; twist wire ends together and form into a loop at back of wreath. Overlap ends of felt tubes.

4. Use tracing paper to make snowman, nose, and snowflake patterns (pg. 123).

5. For snowmen, use patterns to cut twelve body shapes (six fronts and six backs) from ecru felt and six noses from orange felt.

6. Glue one nose to each snowman front. Use three strands of floss to work Satin Stitch for eyes and Running Stitch for mouths.

7. Leaving an opening for stuffing, glue edges of each snowman front and back together. Lightly stuff each snowman with fiberfill. Glue each opening closed.

8. For each snowman scarf, tear a $3/4$" x 8" strip of flannel; tie around neck.

(Continued on page 102)

CHRISTMAS MEMORIES ALBUM

WHAT TO BUY

Photo album (ours measures
   10" x 11¾")
³/₈ yd 72"w green felt
Two red felt pieces
White, peach, and red acrylic
   paint
White baby rickrack
   (4-yd package)

THINGS YOU HAVE AT HOME

Tracing paper, black felt-tip pen,
paintbrushes, transfer paper,
stylus, uncoated floral wire, wire
cutters, buttons, and glue

TECHNIQUES YOU'LL NEED

Making Patterns (pg. 104)
Painting Tips (pg. 105)

Featuring a portrait of the jolly elf, this organizer for holiday photos is so enchanting and economical that you'll want to make several — one for yourself and more to share with friends! Start by covering a photo album with felt, then paint the Santa pattern on the front and finish with three-dimensional touches, including wire spectacles, bright buttons, and baby rickrack.

COVERED PHOTO ALBUM

1. Measure width and height of open album; add 4" to each measurement. Cut a piece of green felt the determined measurements.

2. Center open album on felt piece. Glue corners of felt over corners of album. Trimming felt to fit around album hardware, glue edges of felt over edges of album.

3. To cover inside of album, cut two 2"w green felt strips 2" shorter than height of album. Center and glue one strip along each side of album hardware with one long edge tucked under album hardware.

4. Cut two red felt pieces ½" smaller on all sides than album front. Glue felt pieces inside front and back of album.

5. Use tracing paper to make Santa pattern (pg. 127). Leaving enough room for words, center pattern on album front. Draw around pattern with black pen.

6. Basecoat entire design with white paint. (It may take several coats of paint to cover design area.)

7. Transfer remaining lines of design to painted area. Refer to color key (pg. 127) to paint remainder of design.

8. Transfer "Christmas Memories" pattern (this page) to album. Paint transferred words white.

9. Transfer eyes to Santa. Use black pen to color eyes, draw over transferred lines, and outline hat, beard, mustache, and eyebrows. Paint white highlights in eyes.

10. Bend a 12" length of wire into shape of spectacles (**Fig. 1**). Poke wire ends through felt on each side of head.

Fig. 1

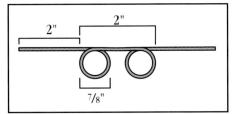

11. Glue rickrack 1" from each edge of album front. Glue buttons to hat and at corners of album.

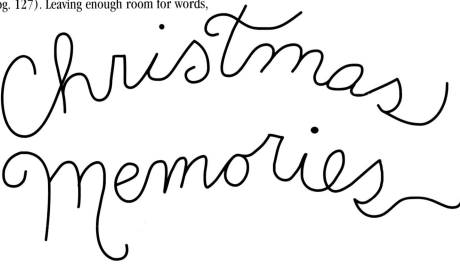

FESTIVE PLACE MATS

WHAT TO BUY

Two bottles of white and one
  bottle each of red and green
  acrylic paint
1/2"w removable tape
Compressed craft sponge

THINGS YOU HAVE AT HOME

Vinyl flooring scraps (can be
found at flooring supply stores or
discount outlets), utility knife,
yardstick, paintbrushes, acetate,
permanent felt-tip pen, craft knife,
cutting mat, pencil with an unused
eraser, and non-toxic matte
acrylic spray sealer

TECHNIQUES YOU'LL NEED

Painting Tips (pg. 105)

*A*dd festivity to brunches,
*lunches, and dinners by decorating
your table with these holiday place
mats. Fashioned from scraps of vinyl
flooring, six can be made for under
$10! Use sponge stencils to produce
the graceful holly border that contrasts
pleasantly with the checkerboard motif.*

Fig. 1

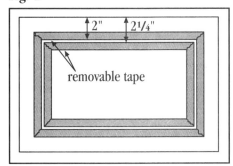

2"   2¼"

removable tape

STENCILED PLACE MATS

1. For each place mat, use utility knife to
cut a 12" x 18" piece of vinyl flooring.
Allowing to dry between coats, basecoat
back of vinyl flooring piece (front of place
mat) with two coats of white paint.

2. For red border, place removable tape on
place mat as shown in **Fig. 1**. Paint ¹/₄"w
space between tape edges red. Allow to dry;
remove tape.

3. Use checkerboard and holly and
ribbon border patterns (pg. 127) to make
stencils. Use sponge pieces to stencil red
checkerboard on corners of place mat and
green holly and ribbon border along outer
border of place mat.

4. Use pencil eraser to stamp red dots
between ribbon lengths; use paintbrush to
paint red lines along sides of checkerboard
corners.

5. Spray place mat with sealer.

SPIRITED YULE STONES

HAT TO BUY

Santa Rock:
White, peach, red, green, and black acrylic paint

Snowman Rock:
White, orange, red, green, and black acrylic paint

THINGS YOU HAVE AT HOME

Two rocks with smooth, flat surfaces large enough for desired design, tracing paper, transfer paper, stylus, paintbrushes, black permanent felt-tip pen, and clear acrylic spray sealer

TECHNIQUES YOU'LL NEED

Making Patterns (pg. 104)
Painting Tips (pg. 105)

*S*pruce up a windowsill, desktop, or lonely nook with these spirited Yule stones. They could put even Scrooge into a festive mood! Acrylic paints and easy patterns transform flat stones into delightful paperweights and more.

PAINTED ROCKS

1. Transfer outlines of patterns (pg. 123) to rocks.

2. Refer to color key (pg. 123) to paint designs.

3. Use pen to outline painted areas, draw details, and draw over transferred lines. For snowman, use pen to write "Need More Snow" on sign.

4. Spray rocks with two to three coats of sealer.

FOLKSY FELT STOCKINGS
(Continued from page 88)

SNOWMAN AND DOG STOCKING

1. Use tracing paper to make stocking pattern (pg. 125). Use pattern to cut one stocking from black felt.

2. Use patterns (pg. 122) to make snowman, arms, nose, hat, and dog appliqués from felt.

3. Arrange and fuse appliqués on stocking front.

4. Use zigzag stitch and black thread to machine stitch appliqués in place.

5. Use three strands of grey floss to work Straight Stitches for snowflakes on snowman and three strands of ecru floss to work remaining snowflakes.

6. Use black thread to work Running Stitch for mouth and Cross Stitches for eyes on snowman; work Straight Stitches for nose and eyes on dog.

7. Follow Steps 7 - 10 of **Tree and Cat Stocking** instructions to finish stocking, using green felt piece for stocking back.

ELEGANT MOSAIC BALLS
(Continued from page 90)

6. In bowl, mix black paint with a small amount of spackling compound until compound is dark grey (we used about $1/4$ teaspoon of paint for each tablespoon of compound). For easier workability, allow compound to stand 30 minutes before applying to ball. Working on a small area at a time, use fingers to apply spackling compound to ball, pressing compound between mosaic pieces. When spaces are filled, rub fingers over surface of ball to remove any excess compound. Use a lightly dampened sponge piece to gently clean residue from mosaic pieces; allow to dry. Apply additional coats of spackling compound to ball as needed to build compound up to the same level as mosaic pieces.

7. Allowing to dry between coats, apply several coats of sealer to ornament.

8. For each hanger, fold an 8" length of ribbon in half to form a loop. Use straight pin to attach ends of ribbon to ornament.

PLAID FOREST TREE SKIRT
(Continued from page 91)

skirt opening. Use clear nylon thread and zigzag stitch to machine stitch edges of bias strip to skirt.

5. Use patterns (pg. 121) to make tree appliqués from fabrics. Arrange and fuse appliqués on tan felt pieces. Leaving a $1/4$" tan felt border, cut out appliqués.

6. Arrange trees on tree skirt; pin in place. Using clear thread and a zigzag stitch, machine stitch along edges of appliqués.

7. Use three strands of floss to work Straight Stitches for snowflakes. Knotting and trimming floss at front of some buttons, use six strands of floss to sew buttons to tree skirt border and to trees.

JOLLY SNOWMAN ORNAMENTS
(Continued from page 96)

4. Paint hats and pebbles black.

5. For hanger, use thumbtack to punch a hole in center bottom of can. Cut an 8" length of clear thread, fold in half, and thread ends through hole in bottom of can; glue to inside of can.

6. For noses, use pattern made in Step 2 to cut circle from orange felt. Cut felt circle into quarters. Roll each quarter into a cone and glue edge to secure; trim large end flat.

7. For each bow tie, cut a 2" x $3^1/4$" red felt strip for bow and a $3/4$" x 2" strip for bow center. Pinching bow at center, wrap bow center around bow; glue to secure.

8. For each snowman, glue pebbles to ball for eyes and mouth, pressing pebbles into foam slightly. Glue hat, nose, and bow tie to head, pressing nose slightly to wrinkle.

EASY WINTER WREATH
(Continued from page 97)

9. Use patterns to cut four snowflakes and four snowflake centers from ecru felt.

10. Place one snowflake center on each snowflake. Stitching through both layers, use pearl cotton thread to work Straight Stitches and French Knots on each snowflake center.

11. For bow, tear a 3" x 20" piece of flannel. Glue short ends together to form a loop. Tear a 3" x 35" piece of flannel and tie into a bow around center of loop.

12. Glue snowmen, snowflakes, and bow to wreath; glue button to bow.

The Well-Stocked
CRAFT ROOM

*A*s clever crafters all know, you can save lots of time and money on a project when you keep a good variety of general supplies on hand. A well-stocked craft room is something that evolves as you collect leftover dabs of paint or scraps of fabric and take advantage of sales. Our editors checked their own workrooms, compared notes, and compiled this handy list of frequently needed items to help you plan your ideal craft room.

Buttons
Cardboard: heavy (corrugated),
   lightweight (poster board),
   tagboard (manila folders)
Chalk
Cotton string
Craft sticks
Crayons
Crochet hooks
Cutting mat (or folded
   newspaper or cardboard)
Embroidery floss
Embroidery hoop
Fabric scraps
Felt scraps
Floral wire: coated, uncoated
Fusible products: paper-backed
   web and web tape,
   interfacing
Glue: craft, craft glue stick,
   fabric, decoupage, hot or
   low-temperature glue gun,
   rubber cement,
   spray adhesive
Hole punch
Ink pad: black
Iron
Ironing board

Jute twine
Knives: craft, utility
Measuring tools: ruler, yardstick,
   tape measure
Needles: sewing, embroidery,
   tapestry, large tapestry
Paint: acrylic, dimensional, gold
   paint pen
Paintbrushes: round, flat, liner,
   fan, foam, stencil
Paper: tracing, white tissue, white
   typing, stationery, card stock,
   construction
Pencils: #2 pencil, colored, fabric
   marking, chalk, grease
Pens: colored felt-tip, black
   permanent felt-tip, removable
   fabric marking pen
Pins: straight, safety
Polyester batting
Polyester fiberfill
Pressing cloth
Raffia
Ribbon: scraps, curling
Scissors: multi-purpose, craft,
   fabric shears, pinking shears,
   small sharp embroidery

Sealer: clear acrylic spray
Sewing machine
Spanish moss
Sponges: compressed craft,
   small sponge pieces
Stapler
Stylus (or ball-point pen that
   doesn't write)
T-shirt form (or cardboard
   covered with waxed paper)
Tape: transparent, masking,
   removable
Tear-away stabilizer (fusible or
   non-fusible) or medium
   weight paper
Thread: sewing (to match
   fabrics), clear nylon
Tools: wire cutters, needle-nose
   pliers, handsaw, large nail
Transfer paper: graphite
   transfer paper, dressmakers'
   tracing paper
Translucent vinyl template
   material
Yarn scraps

TECHNIQUES

TIPS ON ADHESIVES

When using any adhesive, carefully follow the manufacturer's instructions.

White craft glue: Recommended for paper. Dry flat.

Tacky craft glue: Recommended for paper, fabric, floral, or wood. Dry flat or secure items with clothespins or straight pins until glue is dry.

Craft glue stick: Recommended for paper or for gluing small, lightweight items to paper or another surface. Dry flat.

Fabric glue: Recommended for fabric or paper. Dry flat or secure items with clothespins or straight pins until glue is dry.

Decoupage glue: Recommended for decoupaging fabric or paper to a surface such as wood or glass. Use purchased decoupage glue or mix one part craft glue with one part water.

Hot or low-temperature glue gun: Recommended for floral, paper, fabric, or wood. Hold in place until set. A low-temperature glue gun is safer than a hot glue gun, but the bond made with the glue is not as strong.

Rubber cement: Recommended for paper and cardboard. May discolor photos; may discolor paper with age. Dry flat (dries very quickly).

Spray adhesive: Recommended for paper or fabric. Can be repositionable or permanent. Dry flat.

MAKING PATTERNS

Note: To make a more durable pattern, use tracing paper pattern to draw design onto translucent vinyl template material; cut out.

Whole patterns: Place tracing paper over pattern and trace; cut out.

Half-patterns: Fold tracing paper in half, place fold along dashed line, and trace pattern half; turn folded paper over and draw over traced lines on remaining side. Unfold pattern; cut out.

Two-part patterns: Trace one part of pattern onto tracing paper. Match dotted line and arrows of traced part with dotted line and arrows of second part in book and trace second part. Repeat until entire pattern is traced; cut out.

Transferring patterns: Make a tracing paper pattern. Position pattern on project. Place transfer paper, coated side down between pattern and project. Use a stylus to trace over lines of pattern.

FUSING BASICS

Using fusible web: (**Note:** To protect your ironing board, cover with muslin. Web material that sticks to iron may be removed with hot iron cleaner, available at fabric and craft stores.) Place web side of paper-backed fusible web on wrong side of fabric. Follow manufacturer's instructions to fuse web to fabric. Remove paper backing. Position fusible fabric, web side down, on project and press with heated iron for ten seconds. Repeat, lifting and overlapping iron until all fusing is complete.

Making fusible fabric appliqués: (**Note:** When fusing a light-colored fabric over a dark or print fabric, line light-colored fabric with fusible interfacing before applying web.)

Trace appliqué pattern onto paper side of web. When making more than one appliqué, leave at least 1" between shapes on web. Cutting 1/2" outside drawn shape, cut out web shape. Fuse to wrong side of fabric. Cut out shape along drawn lines. Remove paper backing. If pattern is a half-pattern or to make a reversed appliqué, make a tracing paper pattern (turn traced pattern over for reversed appliqué) and follow instructions using traced pattern.

Foil method: When applying fusible web to items with holes or items that are narrow (lace, ribbon, or doilies), place a piece of foil, shiny side up, under items to prevent web from sticking to ironing board. Place item(s), wrong side up, on foil. Place web, paper side up, over item; press. Peel item(s) from foil; trim excess web. Remove paper backing and fuse to project.

STITCHED APPLIQUÉS

Stitching appliqués: Place paper or stabilizer on wrong side of background fabric under fused appliqué.

Beginning on a straight edge of appliqué if possible, position project under presser foot so that most of stitching will be on appliqué. Take a stitch in fabric and bring bobbin thread to top. Hold both threads toward you and sew over them for several stitches to secure. Stitch over all exposed raw edges of appliqué(s) and along detail lines as indicated in instructions.

When stitching is complete, remove stabilizer. Clip threads close to stitching.

PAINTING TIPS

Transferring a painting pattern to project: Make a tracing paper pattern. Position pattern on project. Place transfer paper, coated side down between pattern and project. Use a stylus to trace over lines of pattern. If painting a transferred design that has basecoat with details on top, transfer the outlines of the basecoat to project first and paint basecoat, then transfer and paint details.

Basecoat: Use a flat paintbrush or foam brush to paint an entire item or an outlined area on an item with an even coat of paint; two or three coats may be necessary to completely cover the item or area.

Highlights: Use a liner, small round, or flat paintbrush to paint a lighter area of paint (usually white or off-white) on the basecoat, giving the appearance of light.

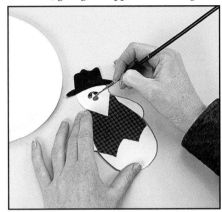

Dots: Dip the tip of a round paintbrush, the handle end of a paintbrush, or one end of a toothpick in paint and touch to project. Dip in paint each time for uniform dots.

Painting with a sponge shape: Use a permanent pen to draw around pattern on a dry compressed craft sponge; cut out sponge shape. Dampen sponge shape to expand. Pour a small amount of paint onto a paper plate. Dip one side of sponge shape into paint and remove excess on a paper towel. Lightly press sponge shape on project, then carefully lift. Reapplying paint to sponge shape as necessary, repeat to paint additional shapes on project.

Stenciling: For stencil, cut a piece of template material at least 1" larger on all sides than pattern. Place template material directly over pattern in book. Use a permanent pen to trace pattern onto template material. Place template material on cutting mat and use craft knife to cut out stencil, making sure edges are smooth.

Pour a small amount of paint onto a paper plate. Hold or tape (using removable tape) stencil in place on project. Dip a stencil brush or sponge piece in paint and remove excess on a paper towel. Brush or sponge should be almost dry to produce good results. Beginning at edge of cutout area, apply paint in a stamping motion over stencil. Carefully remove stencil from project. To stencil a design in reverse, clean stencil and turn stencil over.

Sealing: If an item will be handled frequently or used outdoors, we recommend sealing the item with clear acrylic sealer. Sealers are available in spray or brush-on form in several finishes. Follow manufacturer's instructions to apply sealer.

Painting with dimensional paint: Turn bottle upside down to fill tip before each use. While painting, clean tip often with a paper towel. If tip becomes clogged, insert a straight pin into opening to unclog.

To paint, touch tip to project. Squeezing and moving bottle steadily, apply paint to project, being careful not to flatten paint line. If securing an appliqué, center line of paint to cover raw edge of appliqué. If painting detail lines, center line of paint over transferred line on project or freehand details as desired.

To correct a mistake, use a paring knife to gently scrape excess paint from project before it dries. Carefully remove stain with non-acetone nail polish remover on a cotton swab. A mistake may also be camouflaged by incorporating it into the design.

EMBROIDERY STITCHES

Straight Stitch: Referring to Fig. 1, bring needle up at 1 and go down at 2 as desired.

Fig. 1

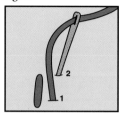

Running Stitch: Referring to Fig. 2, make a series of straight stitches with stitch length equal to the space between stitches.

Fig. 2

Backstitch: Referring to Fig. 3, bring needle up at 1; go down at 2; bring up at 3 and pull through. For next stitch, insert needle at 1; bring up at 4 and pull through.

Fig. 3

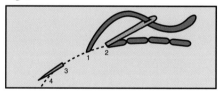

Cross Stitch: Referring to Fig. 4, bring needle up at 1; go down at 2. Bring needle up at 3; go down at 4. Repeat for each stitch.

Fig. 4

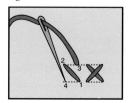

Blanket Stitch: Referring to Figs. 5 and 6, bring needle up at 1. Keeping thread below point of needle, go down at 2 and come up at 3. Continue working as shown.

Fig. 5   Fig. 6

French Knot: Referring to Fig. 7, bring needle up at 1. Wrap floss once around needle and insert needle at 2, holding end of floss with non-stitching fingers. Tighten knot, then pull needle through fabric, holding floss until it must be released. For a larger knot, use more strands; wrap only once.

Fig. 7

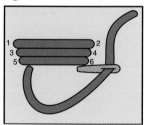

Satin Stitch: Referring to Fig. 8, come up at odd numbers and go down at even numbers with the stitches touching but not overlapping.

Fig. 8

PATTERNS

PAINTSTITCHED PILLOW

VALENTINE VASES

PATTERNS (continued)

HEARTS

A

B

C

D

E

F

G

H

HAT

BEARD

FACE

LEPRECHAUN MAGNETS

POT OF GOLD MAGNETS

BACK

COINS

FRONT

CROSS

EGG

EASTER SUN CATCHERS

FENCEROW RABBITS

PATTERNS (continued)

JELLY BEAN DAISY BAGS

LEAF

EASTER SUN CATCHERS

PERKY TABLE RUNNER

FENCEROW RABBITS

Constitutional Cozy

We hold these truths to be self-evident, that ALL MEN are created EQUAL, that they are endowed by their Creator with certain UNALIENABLE RIGHTS, that among these are LIFE, LIBERTY and the pursuit of HAPPINESS.

Festive Fourth Swag

Ohio Star

SQUARE

STAR

Quilter's Flag T-Shirt

PATTERNS (continued)

SPIRITED UNCLE SAM

HAT

FACE

MUSTACHE

EPAULET

BEARD

HAND

SHIRT

STAR

SPECTACULAR TEE

BANNER

God Bless America

FESTIVE FOURTH SWAG
SPECTACULAR TEE

STAR

SPIRITED UNCLE SAM
(cont.)

SHOES

PANTS

113

PATTERNS (continued)

GHOULISH GOODY BUCKETS
BEWITCHING BAGS

PATCHES

STAR

NOSE

HAND

ENCHANTING WITCH

GOBLIN DOOR HANGER

EYE

TRICKS

NOSE

LEAF

MOUTH

PATTERNS (continued)

GOBLIN DOOR HANGER
(cont.)

"NO"

BEWITCHING BAGS

HAT

CIRCLE

CONE

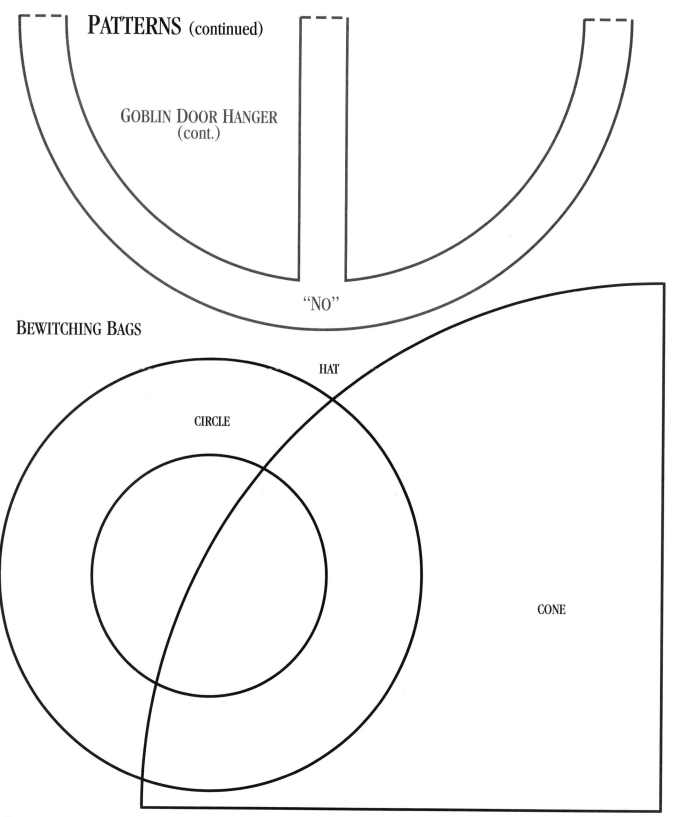

"BOO-GIE" T-SHIRT

CREATIVE
HALLOWEEN CANS

MAGNETIC
JACK-O'-LANTERN

TABLE RUNNER

PUMPKIN-PATCH
PULLOVER

STEM

MEDIUM PUMPKIN

CREATIVE
HALLOWEEN CANS

PUMPKIN

GHOST

PATTERNS (continued)

CANDY CORN

SMALL LEAF

STEM

SMALL PUMPKIN

STEM

STEM

LARGE PUMPKIN

LARGE LEAF

TABLE RUNNER

PUMPKIN-PATCH PULLOVER

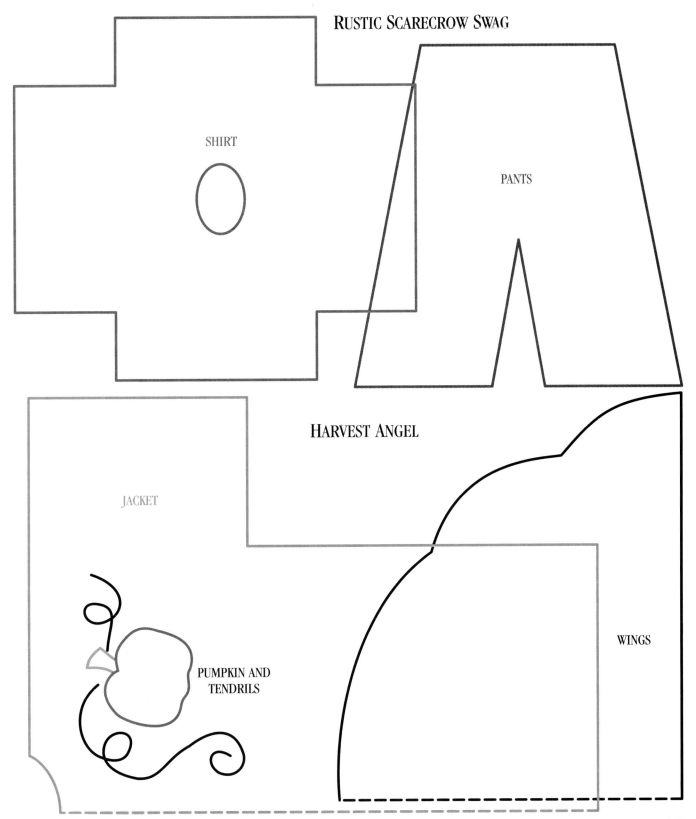

RUSTIC SCARECROW SWAG

SHIRT

PANTS

HARVEST ANGEL

JACKET

WINGS

PUMPKIN AND
TENDRILS

119

PATTERNS (continued)

MAPLE LEAF COASTER SET

AUTUMN APRON

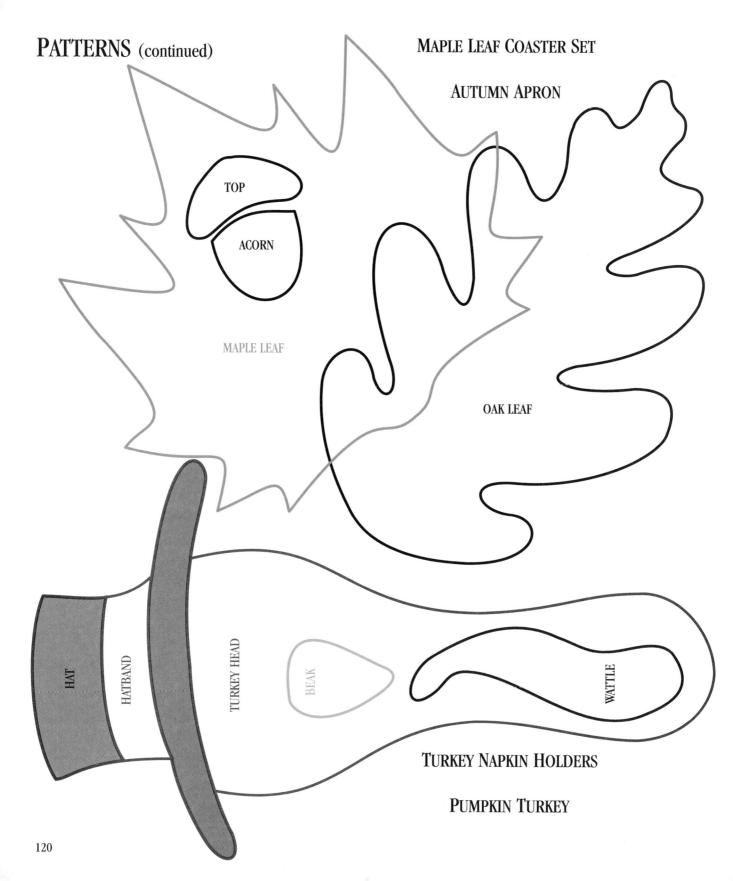

TOP

ACORN

MAPLE LEAF

OAK LEAF

HAT

HATBAND

TURKEY HEAD

BEAK

WATTLE

TURKEY NAPKIN HOLDERS

PUMPKIN TURKEY

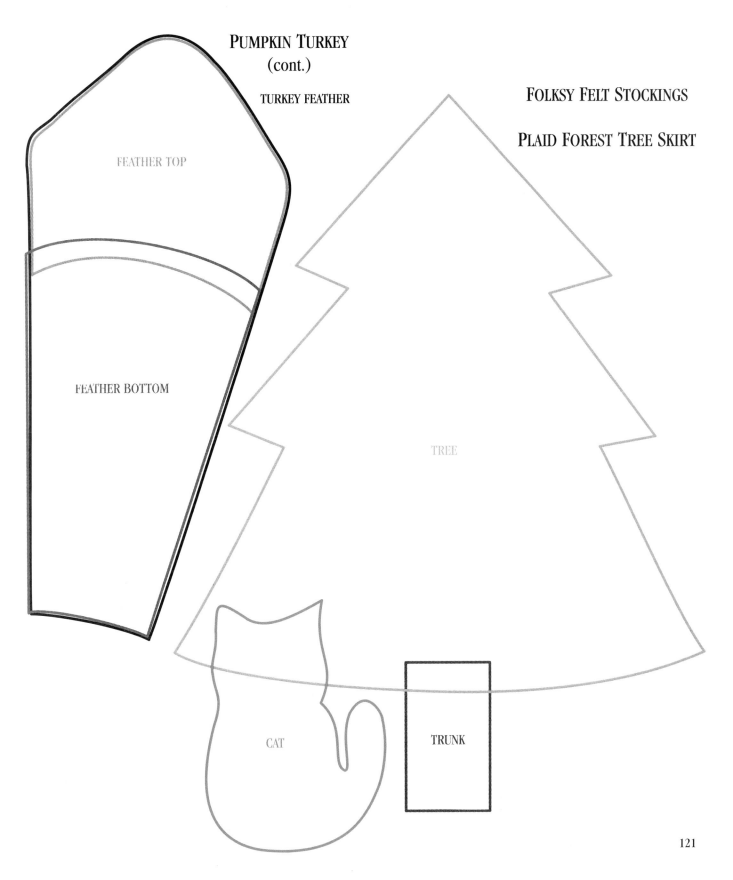

PUMPKIN TURKEY
(cont.)

TURKEY FEATHER

FEATHER TOP

FEATHER BOTTOM

FOLKSY FELT STOCKINGS

PLAID FOREST TREE SKIRT

TREE

CAT

TRUNK

PATTERNS (continued)

RUSTIC COASTER SET

FOLKSY FELT STOCKINGS

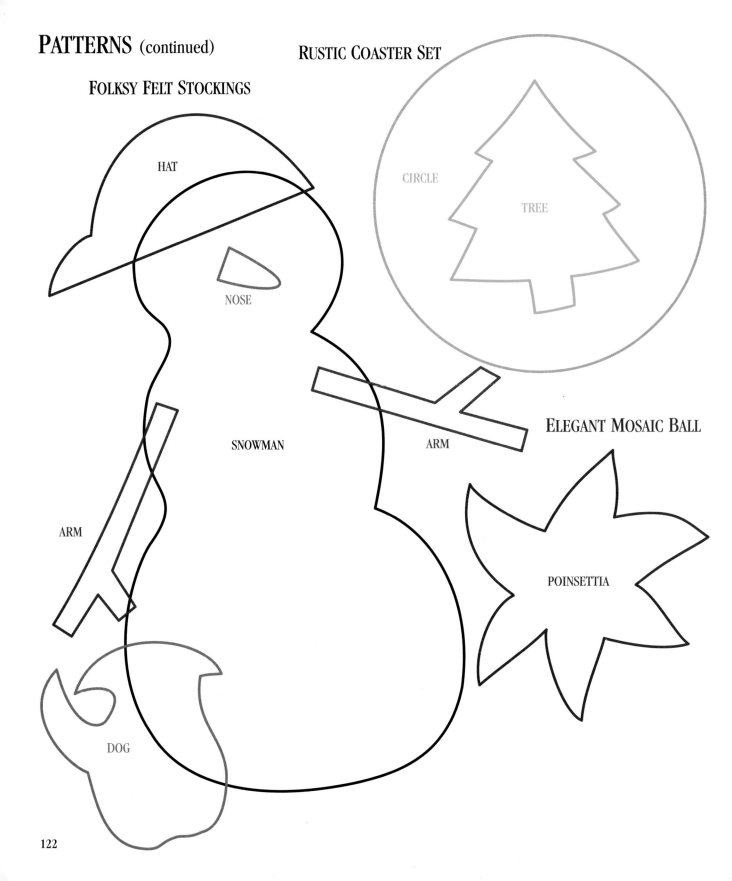

HAT

NOSE

CIRCLE

TREE

SNOWMAN

ARM

ARM

ELEGANT MOSAIC BALL

POINSETTIA

DOG

EASY WINTER WREATH

SNOWFLAKE

CENTER

SNOWMAN

SPIRITED YULE STONES

COLOR KEY

- ☐ White
- ☐ Peach
- ■ Red
- ■ Orange
- ■ Light Green
- ■ Green
- ■ Grey
- ■ Black

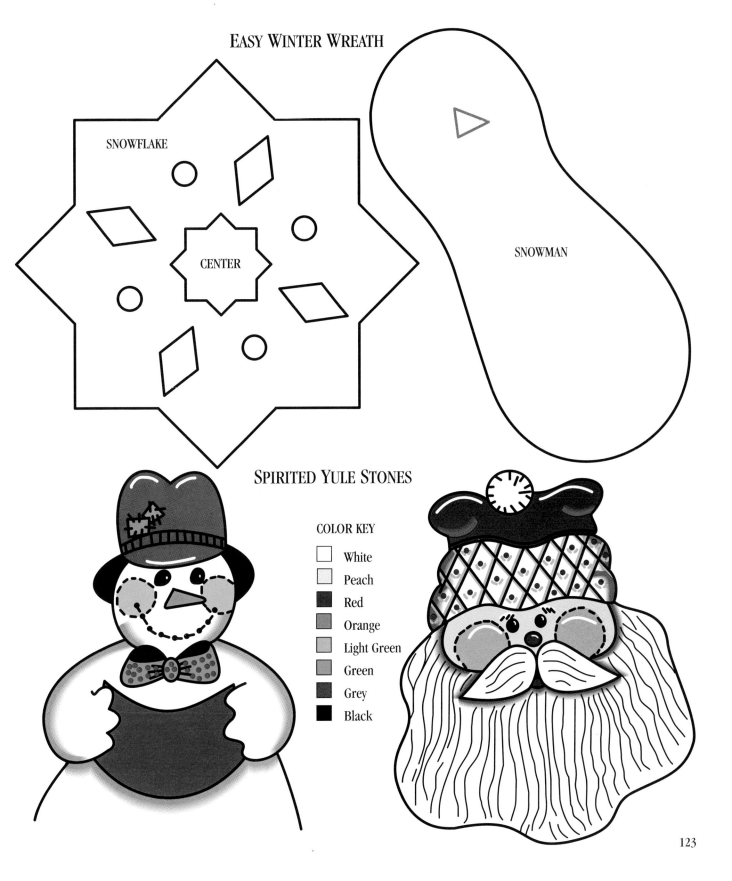

PATTERNS (continued)

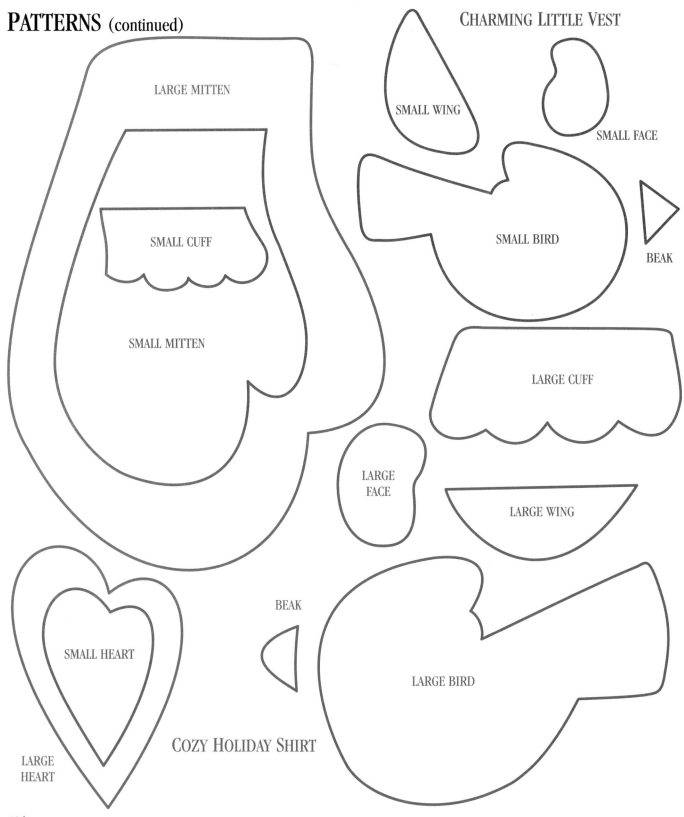

LARGE MITTEN

CHARMING LITTLE VEST

SMALL WING

SMALL FACE

SMALL CUFF

SMALL BIRD

BEAK

SMALL MITTEN

LARGE CUFF

LARGE FACE

LARGE WING

SMALL HEART

BEAK

LARGE BIRD

COZY HOLIDAY SHIRT

LARGE HEART

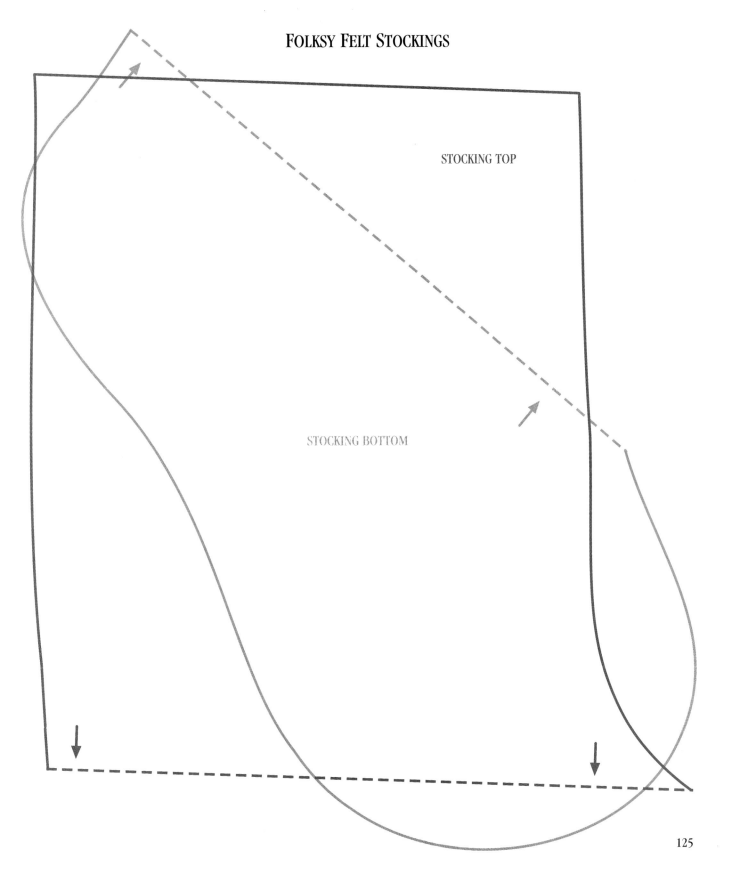

STOCKING TOP

STOCKING BOTTOM

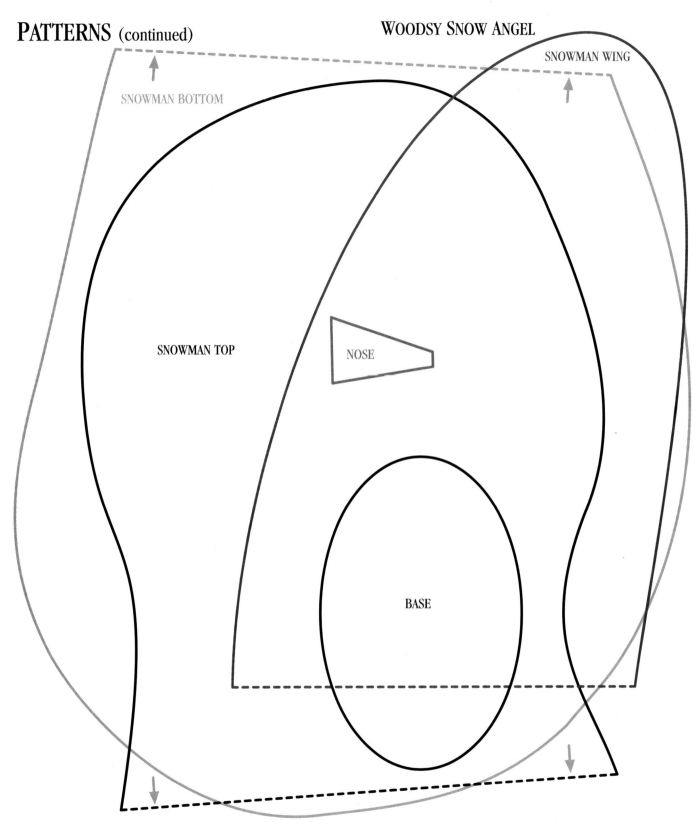

SNOWMAN WING

SNOWMAN BOTTOM

SNOWMAN TOP

NOSE

BASE

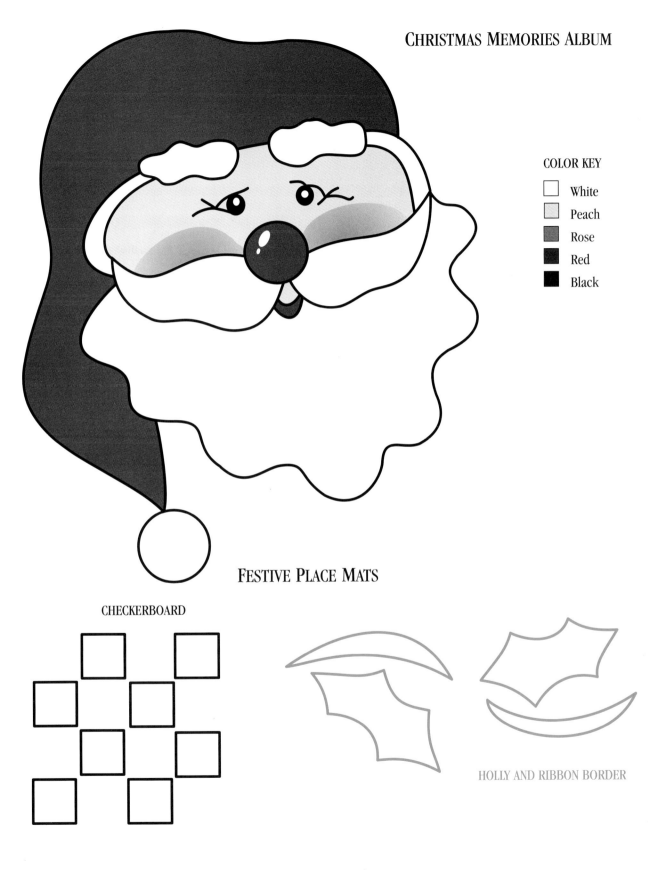

COLOR KEY

- White
- Peach
- Rose
- Red
- Black

FESTIVE PLACE MATS

CHECKERBOARD

HOLLY AND RIBBON BORDER

CREDITS

We want to extend a warm *thank you* to the generous people who allowed us to photograph our projects in their homes: James and Joan Adams, Dr. Dan and Sandra Cook, Dennis and Tricia Hendrix, Ellison and Joe Madden, Charles and Peg Mills, Duncan and Nancy Porter, Dr. Reed and Becky Thompson, and Paul and Ann Weaver.

To Magna IV Color Imaging of Little Rock, Arkansas, we say thank you for the superb color reproduction and excellent pre-press preparation.

We especially want to recognize photographers David Hale, Mark Mathews, Larry Pennington, Karen Shirey, and Ken West of Peerless Photography, and Jerry R. Davis of Jerry Davis Photography, all of Little Rock, Arkansas, for their time, patience, and excellent work.

We extend a special word of thanks to Conn Baker Gibney, who designed the *Elegant Mosaic Balls* shown on page 90.

Leisure Arts would like to thank Viking Husqvarna Sewing Machine Company of Cleveland, Ohio, for providing the sewing machines used to make some of the projects in this book.